John T. Wayland

PLANNING CONGREGATIONAL WORSHIP SERVICES

BROADMAN PRESS
Nashville, Tennessee

To My Wife
Who lives the worshiping life
in creative love of
God and neighbor

© Copyright 1971 • Broadman Press
All rights reserved
4223–08
ISBN: 0–8054–2308–7

Library of Congress Catalog Card Number: 72–1708067
Dewey Decimal Classification: 264
Printed in the United States of America

PREFACE

Worship is the first and most important function of the local church. Like the individual Christian, her primary purpose is to "glorify God and to enjoy him forever." Yet many of our churches have services which are dull and uninspiring. Some of them are mainly promotional efforts at maintaining the church's activities and its financial status. Too many people, especially youth and young adults, are deserting the worship services, and are looking to strange cults, oriental religions, or humanitarian movements for satisfaction of their spiritual hungers.

The Christian church as a whole possesses a rich heritage of worship practices, most of which needs rediscovering. Each denomination has a vital tradition which can be revitalized. In addition we are living in a time of tremendous experimentation in ways of worshiping our God. The Holy Spirit is undoubtedly in some of these fresh breezes. His is a history of startling innovations in ways of winning and growing men. We must be alert and ready to follow that which he blesses, testing every spirit by the spirit of Christ.

This book is a small effort at helping our churches and their pastors, worship committees, and planning teams find the best ways of worship as they endeavor to be and to do what God wants them to be and do in a time of lost and confused people.

We are deeply indebted to the patient people who have taught us what we know about worship, including the churches of which we have been pastor (First Baptist Church, Monroe, North Carolina, Temple Baptist Church, Durham, North Carolina, Pimlico Baptist Church, Baltimore, Maryland, and First Baptist Church, North Wilkesboro, North Carolina) and interim pastor and the seminary where we are now privileged to teach. We are grateful to many fellow ministers who have shared with us their ideas and suggestions. These include many pastors and students. The most recent help has come from Reverend R. F. Smith, Jr., pastor, First Baptist Church, Durham, North Carolina, and Reverend Allen Laymon, pastor, First Baptist Church, North Wilkesboro, North Carolina. The several orders of service given in this volume are the contributions of many friends, to whom we owe a great debt.

Mrs. Charles Carter, capable and efficient secretary to the faculty at Southeastern Baptist Theological Seminary, has given capable and helpful service in the typing and preparation of the manuscript.

JOHN T. WAYLAND
1970

CONTENTS

1   The Nature and Purpose of Worship   1

2   Enriching and Planning Worship Services   20

3   Planning Special Worship Services   31

4   Planning Other Special Services   44

5   Arranging and Printing Orders of Worship   52

6   Conducting and Evaluating Worship Services   56

   A Selected Bibliography   63

   Resources   69

1

The Nature and Purpose of Worship

We worship because it is our nature. We can't help it. We're made that way. Everyone worships something or someone. It may be an idol, or the Eternal God, or himself. "He gave his life to the making of money" is a statement about worship.

When Paul spoke on Mars Hill after taking a tour of Athens, he remarked upon the many gods which the Athenians worshiped. There was Venus, the goddess of sex; Mars, the god of brute force; Mercury, of sharp business practices; Bacchus, of revelry; and many others including the one he specifically mentioned, the vague general obeisance to religion—the "Unknown God." Would you say that although we have made no images of them, we Americans are more devoted to these pagan gods than the Athenians were? As measured by the amount of time, energy, and money we give them? They still give us their "call to worship": "This is the life. Come on, live it up!" The end is the mockery of life, not life at all, but death. Sometimes the "Death of a Salesman." These false gods are just devils.

The Object of Our Worship

The true God calls us to life with a capital *L*. His Incarnate Son still invites, "I have come in order that they might have life, life in all its fulness" (John 10:10, TEV). His revelation of the God worthy of our worship is unique—the only one of its kind. The Son emptied himself of his divine nature and made himself one of us, sharing with us in our human predicament and daring with us in our half-lighted adventure. He went about doing good to all who needed help, including those who were mean to him. Having called some to himself he loved them creatively, drawing forth from them the best that the Father of love and grace had put into them.

Of his own free will this Son of God gave himself to cruel men to do with him as they would, and when they killed him he begged the Supreme Judge to let them go free. As he made plans to go home, he invited one who was nearby to go with him. He would have taken others if they had had their bags packed with repentance and faith.

"Therefore God has highly exalted him and bestowed on him the name which is above every name, that at the name of Jesus every knee should bow, in heaven and on earth and under the earth, and every tongue confess that Jesus Christ is Lord, to the glory of God the Father" (Phil. 2:9-11, RSV). What else can we do but worship this Christ?

The dynamic connection between Christian worship and the Christian life-style is explosively apparent in the same passage from *Today's English Version,* starting with the fifth verse:

> The attitude you should have is the one that Christ Jesus had:
> He always had the very nature of God,
> But he did not think that by force he should try to become equal with God.
> Instead, of his own free will he gave it all up,
> And took the nature of a servant.
> He became like man, he appeared in human likeness;
> He was humble and walked the path of obedience to death—his death on the cross.
> For this reason God raised him to the highest place above,
> And gave him the name that is greater than any other name,
> So that, in honor of the name of Jesus, all beings in heaven, and on earth, and in the world below
> Will fall on their knees,
> And all will openly proclaim that Jesus Christ is the Lord,
> To the glory of God the Father.

In the Bible worship is closely tied to ethics and evangelism. Isaiah saw the Lord in all his glory. His own unworthiness was devastating in the presence of such worth. His beloved nation was not worth saving. He himself was "sunk." But the holy God could use such a repentant, humble, teachable spirit. He "made it right"—cleansed him of his sin. It was then, and only then, that Isaiah heard the call to evangelism and missions. Only then was he ready to go. Apparently the anguished cry for missionaries had gone unheeded. No one would go. They hadn't seen the Lord, or if they had, they had not worshiped him.

Worship in the New Testament Churches

For the New Testament churches, worship was essentially corporate. At Pentecost "all the believers were gathered together in one place." It was only then that the Holy Spirit came. Private devotions have a very important place in the life of the Christian and of the church. They are, however, complementary rather than primary. The Christian approaches God through Christ. To be "in Christ" is to be a part of his body, which is the worshiping church.

When the Spirit came at Pentecost, he gave a power the likeness of which has never again been equaled. Not only did the Galileans speak in many languages, but more remarkably, each language was used for one purpose: the praise of a wonderful God. To a questioning audience Peter told the good news that God had fulfilled his promise to redeem Israel. That amazingly enough he had done it through a man they had murdered, raising him from the dead and making him Lord and Messiah. God had acted in love and mercy. They had acted in sin and death. God had offered. They had rejected. They must do an about-face in mind and heart and deed. They must believe in this Christ and offer themselves for baptism in his name for the remission of sins, if they wanted to receive the free gift of God. Three thousand of them joyfully accepted the offer of new life. Worship led by the Holy Spirit had broken out into evangelism.

Then followed the whole cycle of Christian action: "They spent their time in learning from the apostles, taking part in the fellowship, and sharing in the fellowship meals and the prayers" (Acts 2:42). Reverential awe settled upon the people as the apostles performed miracles. They pooled their material resources. They worshiped daily in the Temple. They had progressive dinners from house to house in a glorious good time, praising God all the while. The Lord added converts daily.

Worship came first, then evangelism, religious education, fellowship and recreation, Christian love and sharing. It was all religious education, in a sense, because what a church *is* teaches more than what it says. It was all evangelism, in a way, because such living is infectious with an irresistible contagion. It was all fellowship because God had done great things for them, and they were committed to doing great things for him and for each other. It was recreation of the highest order for body, mind, and spirit. Weariness and death had been overcome. It was more than a healthy alternation between work and worship for which we aim today. It was the full experience of work being worship, while worship was reasonable service to Almighty God. All things were brought into subjection to him: material possessions, family ties, religious preferences, national loyalties, and personal ambitions.

Like a great rocket, the church at Pentecost left the launching pad with a power thrust that put her in orbit around the heart of God. Her worship of him was as joyful as it was intense and as free as it was all-pervading. The Spirit was manifest in happy service of God and in loving service to man. Worship and life were practically one. The church was preeminently a fellowship, a fellowship of God with man, of man with man; and Jesus Christ was in the center.

Perhaps it would be well in thinking about worship, in planning experiences of worship, in contemplating the needs of our people, in endeavoring to do the will of God, to look again and again at Pentecost and the short period which followed it. The best was at the first. We are measured by the excellence of that experience of worship and life.

One of the outstanding features of those early worship experiences was that they were *congregational* worship services, the theme of this book. Everyone was in on the act. This was true not because each person demanded a hearing. It rested on solid theological, spiritual foundations of the nature of Christ's ministry, of the gospel, of the ministry of each individual Christian.

Each Christian a Servant and Priest
Christ's ministry was that of servanthood, and he expected that of his followers to be the same. Jesus repeatedly stated that the way to greatness was that of service. For example, when the

disciples argued over positions of authority, he called them together for special instruction about the matter. He told them: "The kings of this world have power over their people, and the rulers are called 'Friends of the People.' But this is not the way it is with you; rather, the greatest one among you must be like the youngest, and the leader must be like the servant. Who is greater, the one who sits down to eat or the one who serves him? The one who sits down, of course. But I am among you as one who serves" (Luke 22:25-27).

Judaism and paganism have priests. In the New Testament priesthood applies to Jesus Christ alone and through him to all members of his church, and never to one of them as distinct from the others. There is without exception a common priesthood, with no laity. God calls the weak of this world and by his grace makes them strong in his service for his glory. The words "priest" and "priesthood" are never applied in the New Testament to the office of ministry as a place of authority. Even in the extensive lists of church officers and activities in 1 Corinthians 12:28-30 and Ephesians 4:11,12 there is no mention of priests.

To state that all who have received the spirit of Christ are his priests is not to say that all have the same gifts or same ministry. There is plenty of evidence of variety at this point. But the New Testament reveals that each and every ministry has in it the idea of service and sacrifice, and not of office and authority. There are, therefore, in the church no special feelings of inferiority or of superiority (1 Cor. 12:14,26), but only joy in the other's gift.

All this is not to argue that the churches of the New Testament had no order, but it is to assert that there was tremendous variety and some contrasts. The Jerusalem church was dependent more on tradition and the Pauline churches on the Spirit. This is not to say that the church in Jerusalem ignored the Spirit, or Paul tradition. It was a matter of emphasis in a given situation. Luke, Matthew, John, the pastoral letters reflect different conceptions of the church. How could it be hardly otherwise? Anyone who travels around visiting churches of the same denomination today is impressed by the fact that each one has a different personality.

And yet what has been written above was found in all the

New Testament churches. Christ was Lord. The apostle's doctrine was authoritative but only in the Spirit and in matters of more practical concern the apostle could be called to account by the church and was subject, like the church, to the leadership of the Holy Spirit. The church recognized gifts of the Spirit. It set aside certain people to definite tasks under the leadership of the Spirit. But all were servants of Jesus Christ. He was the head of the church. The church was usually spoken of as a local gathering managing its own affairs under the leadership of the Holy Spirit.

Baptists and the Priesthood

Baptists' belief in the priesthood of all believers has grown out of their conception of free grace, the necessity for each person to choose the Lord for himself, and the responsibility of each member for priestly acts of evangelism and for the teaching and pastoral care of a needy brother. Each person must make a public witness of his commitment to Christ.

Evelyn Underhill, in her great classic of all books on worship, has written:

> No other Church has insisted, as the Baptists have done, on the centrality of the New Testament connection between baptism and personal faith, the importance of this great symbolic act of surrender to God; on a realistic conversion of the whole life, inward and outward, as the condition of entrance into the Divine Society. Within that Society all are equal, and all are called to the worshipping life; the 'priesthood of every believer' and the impossibility of substituting any liturgical act for personal communion with God and self-offering to God, are cardinal points of Baptist belief.[1]

The doctrine of universal priesthood is also influential on the Baptist teaching concerning the Lord's Supper. It is a spiritual service. The emphasis is on fellowship with Christ and with the company of believers in the local congregation. Its benefits do not depend upon any special priesthood or privileged class. By vote of the church any member may preside at the table. The pastor usually does this, but it is very common for deacons to lead the prayers and they almost always distribute the elements to the people.

The doctrine of the priesthood of all believers is central in Baptist theology. It was stated at the beginning of the seventeenth century by John Smyth and it has been expounded, confirmed, and implemented by his followers ever since with few lapses. In the earliest Baptist congregations there was no pulpit. The table was located in the very center of the group. Extemporaneous prayers, testimonies, amens were heard. It was customary to interpolate comments in the reading of the Scriptures, by members as well as leaders. Baptists pioneered in hymn singing, but most of the best hymns have been composed by others.

About two generations ago many rural Baptist churches, without realizing it, made spectators of their congregations and so neglected the doctrine of the universal priesthood. Everyone who wanted to sing was expected in the choir and the members of this group practiced long and faithfully and performed well as quartets and as a group. Often there were no hymnbooks in the congregation. The preacher put on a terrific performance, talking loud and fast, in a tremendous effort to move the emotions of the people. The deacons had their "amen corner."

Perhaps the greatest threat to the implementation of priestly function by members of the congregation today comes from the size and wealth of our larger churches. An outstanding preacher, assisted by a well-trained staff of ministerial specialists, and supported by several outstanding choirs, some with bells, etc., really put on a show for the rest of us. Does it remind us of the Roman Catholic mass of the Middle Ages? The priests and their several assistants were worshiping for the people—or at least doing for them what they could not do for themselves—in a vast and beautiful cathedral. The monks were in the choir chanting incantations little understood by the people. Do you get the picture? It's one of many problems we'll tackle later on.

Today we are in almost as great a revolution or reformation as that brought about by Luther, Calvin, Zwingli, and others who rebelled against the medieval mass pictured above. All kinds of experimentation and innovation is going on. What is good, and lasting, and worthy of Almighty God and free and responsible men? Only time will tell. Only that which God blesses will last. In the meantime, we will need some guidelines as we plan congregational worship services. What are the qualities of a good worship service?

Qualities of a Good Worship Service

A service of worship must be led by the Spirit of God or it isn't a worship service. "You must realize, then, that no one who is led by God's Spirit can say, 'A curse on Jesus!', and no one can confess 'Jesus is Lord,' unless he is guided by the Holy Spirit. There are different kinds of spiritual gifts, but the same spirit gives them. There are different ways of serving, but the same Lord is served. . . . Each one is given some proof of the Spirit's presence for the good of all" (1 Cor. 12:3-5,7).

The Christians at Corinth apparently were having trouble with their worship services. Aren't we glad they were. It led Paul, under the inspiration of the Holy Spirit, to write about qualities of a good worship service for us, probably unknowingly, as well as for them. Chapters 10 through 14 of his first letter are of special value to us on this subject.

A service of worship led by the Spirit of God in the early churches had a way of getting out of hand since the people were having such a good time in their newly found power. So Paul wrote that another quality of a worship service should be order, propriety, and peace (1 Cor. 14:33,40). If everyone tried to speak at the same time, confusion would break up the meeting. He insisted that people should take turns in praising God. Of course, the quality of propriety will vary from age to age and place to place. Paul commands that women should not speak in church in keeping with the Jewish law forbidding it. Our generation would cause disorder and break the peace over this. Obviously, the question of what's decent and in order should also be judged by other tests, such as honoring God and edifying the church.

The third quality to which we will draw attention is the one just mentioned—edifying the church. Unless the church of the Lord Jesus Christ is helped by what goes on in the service it must be no good. In dealing with the difficult problem of speaking with tongues Paul used this test at least three times in the fourteenth chapter of 1 Corinthians (v. 5,12,26). He says flatly, "Everything must be of help to the church."

The fourth quality is that of an intelligent witness. Religion without emotion is of very little value, if it is not dead. But the Christian religion, beginning with her Lord, has also been a religion of the mind. Jesus added to the Deuteronomic commandment to love God with heart and soul and might, the love of God with the mind. Paul writes at great length (practically all of 1 Cor. 14) in strong support of speaking God's message intelligibly. He does not rule out emotional outbursts of the Spirit, but he says they are of no value unless they can be understood. He writes: "In church worship I would rather speak five words that can be understood, in order to teach others, than speak thousands of words with strange sounds" (v. 19).

A fifth quality of a good worship service is spontaneity and freedom. Like the good life it is a matter of keeping opposing forces in balance. This quality complements "in decency and in order." In his writing to the Corinthians Paul is very evidently seeking such a balance. To the Thessalonians he wrote: "Do not restrain the Holy Spirit; do not despise inspired messages. Put all things to the test: keep what is good" (1 Thess. 5:19-21). He advised his Corinthian friends to plan for two or three persons to give messages. However, if someone in the group suddenly received a word from God the one then speaking should stop and let him have his say (1 Cor. 14:29-31). He went on to say, however, "God has not called us to be disorderly, but peaceful." Of course, Paul's problem was the very opposite from ours. We have difficulty getting anyone to say anything, in a men's Bible class, for example.

A service of worship should also have the quality of a participating and responsible fellowship. "What do I mean, my brothers? When you meet for worship, one man has a hymn, another a teaching, another a revelation from God, another a message with strange sounds, and still another the explanation of what it means. Everything must be of help to the church" (1 Cor. 14:26).

The word "fellowship" has an interesting derivation and meaning. The "ship" in a noun ending signifies a quality or condition of something. "Fellow" comes from two Anglo-Saxon words from which we get "fee" and "lay." A "fellow" is "one laying down money or property for a joint undertaking."

In our services of worship we have a "fellowship" as each person enters into a partnership in the corporate worship of God. The ushers offer Christian love as hosts to the congregation. The organist offers a prelude in preparation for and/or participation in worship. The choir offers music of differing kinds at appropriate places in praise and adoration. A deacon offers a prayer. The pastor gives a sermon. Individuals make offerings of money, of song, and of prayer. God gives of himself in it all and through it all. What a fellowship! Fellowship with responsibility.

Reverence and humility are qualities of worship as natural and as old as man, the "upward looking creature," the Greeks called him. Some show reverence one way and some persons show it in another way. Conservative Jewish men cover their heads in the synagogue. Christian men uncover theirs as an act of reverence. Paul wrote at some length about the proper way for men and women to go to church (1 Cor. 11:4-16). He felt that men should have short hair and uncovered heads. Women should have long hair and hats. He did agree that one could argue about the matter but that "neither we nor the churches of God have any other custom in worship." Habits do change, however, and reverence is primarily a matter of the heart and its attitude.

Every service of worship should have a purpose and probably a theme to give it unity. Years of experience in planning worship services support this necessity. In evangelical churches the subject of the sermon is the key to the thrust of the whole service. The hymns and the music rendered by the choir will support the purpose of the service. This will be more apparent as we engage in the art of planning worship services in a later chapter. It will also stand out in an examination of the sample orders of service given near the end of the book.

Action, progress, movement will characterize a good worship service. It will begin with the people where they are and will carry them along on the wings of the Spirit of God to the heights of where they ought to be. Because of the nature of men and human psychology there will be rise and fall in interest and spiritual attainment. There will be climaxes or high moments. They may well be experienced at different places by different people. The first climax could come in the pastoral prayer, when the man of God lays on the heart of God the deepest longings and gravest needs of all the people. Another climax may come in the singing of a beautiful anthem or solo. In an evangelical church the sermon will reach its highest climax in presenting God's Word of Love to which each one must say yes or no. And the supreme climax would come in the offering of a life for salvation, by the grace of God.

Variety in a service of worship and differing services of worship is a good quality. The lack of variety spells death in almost everything. In some churches the order of service has not varied one iota in twenty-five years. Drowsiness and lethargy are almost inevitable in such a situation. Some churches which are quite critical of ritual have followed just that for years. Perhaps the most universal little ritual in Baptist churches was started about twenty-five years ago. What is it? The deacons come forward during the last stanza of a hymn to take the offering. This is quite all right, but why do it that way for years? Perhaps the pastors got tired of saying the same thing every Sunday, like "The deacons will please come and take the offering." There are hundreds of offertory sentences, mostly from the Bible, which could be used for this purpose and for the educational and devotional uplift of the people.

More will be said about this later, but in general in most churches the order of service should be changed perceptibly every three to six months. We know of one church which has a new order every Sunday and the people like it. This is very unusual and not recommended. Most people would never feel at home in such a situation—just visiting all the time.

There is real value in having an entirely different kind of service on Sunday night as contrasted with the morning. The people who were at the morning service would probably be refreshed—a worthy aim for a worship service and some new people might be attracted by a new approach. A service of worship should be stimulating, challenging, vitalizing.

And to balance the variety, a good service of worship will possess at-homeness and warmth. Most of the people in the world lead lonely lives at some period in their pilgrimage, and some seem to know nothing else. The church is a home for them and "underneath are the everlasting arms." The Christian religion is basically friendship. Jesus said that he called us friends because he had shared God's good news with us. And one of the wonderful things about being a Christian is that when one travels around a great deal he can find a ready-made family of brothers and sisters wherever he finds a church of Friend Jesus.

But it is more than *human* warmth and friendship that is required. Paul urges his Corinthian friends to speak God's message clearly and intelligibly in church so that when a stranger comes in "he will bow down and worship God, confessing, 'Truly God is here with you!' " (1 Cor. 14:25).

And so we won't get too comfortable in the warm and cozy home, one last quality of a good worship service is proposed. The service should call one to higher ground of ethical, moral, and holy living. We all know that is exactly what it's all about, but by nature we would rather sit than climb. We must be doers of the Word and not hearers only. The ones who will be sitting on Christ's right hand on the judgment day will be those persons who have fed the hungry, clothed the naked, etc., and not those who have just called on his name in worship or performed wonderful works before a crowd. We must not just sing about love, but we must love God and people purposefully. We must render a needed service in love or our pious faith or our inspired preaching means nothing. It is significant that Paul's great poem on love comes right in the middle of his discussion about the right way to worship (1 Cor. 13).

Subjective and Objective Worship

One other fundamental thought on worship should be brought to our attention before we begin planning worship services. Too much of our worship is subjective. We go to church because it's good for us. We measure the sermon by how much we enjoyed it. In this TV age we expect the choir to entertain us. Therefore, fundamental questions about worship could be: Who is the audience in a worship service? Whom should we try to please? The answer to both questions is "God."

Obviously this can be overemphasized. We cannot ignore the people. And, being human, we seldom forget ourselves entirely. But in those rare moments when God and God alone is the center of our life and devotion we are truly at worship. The early Christians were not subjectively thinking about themselves. They didn't worship because it would do them good. Their religion was not a system of ethics, primarily, or of philosophy, or of idealism. The worship of Jesus as Lord was the main driving force of Christianity then, even as it should be now. Worship is the supreme and only indispensable activity of the Christian church. "It alone will endure, like the love of God which it expresses, into heaven, when all other activities of the Church have passed away."[2]

NOTES

All Scripture quotations unless otherwise indicated are from *Today's English Version,* copyright American Bible Society 1966.

1. Evelyn Underhill, *Worship* (New York: Harper & Brothers, 1937), p. 302.

2. William Nichols, *Jacob's Ladder: The Meaning of Worship* p. 9.

2

Enriching and Planning Worship Services

The quality of the experiences of worship enjoyed by a congregation is determined more by the quality of leadership in worship given by the pastor than any other single factor. In general, people don't get ahead of their leader in anything. But this is emphatically true of worship. He sets the spiritual tone consciously and unconsciously whether he realizes it or not. The way he looks, the way he acts, and especially the spirit in which he himself worships are extremely important.

Some years ago a pastor of a large church was concerned when a small boy near the front began to cry loudly near the beginning of the service and had to be taken out by his mother. He was surprised as well as startled because he knew the child well and had been impressed by the boy's reverence and attention. So he called the mother after the service and asked if his friend had been taken ill in the service. The mother informed him that the boy's only remark was, "I looked at God this morning and he didn't smile." The pastor had come into the service from a called deacons' meeting in which there had been some sharp divisions. Worry and weariness of spirit were written vividly on his face and the child had gotten the message.

The Pastor's Preparation

This is not to say, of course, that the leader in worship should wear a superficial smile or carry on a civic-club type of banter in cheering up the populace. The point is that he must really worship God in his own way as he leads others to do so. This takes two kinds of preparation, one short range and the other a lifetime.

The service must be well planned. He must know his way and lead with confidence. He should be able to do so because he led the planning. Secondly, he will worship God in keeping with the quality of his own religious experience over the years. The call to be a Christian is more important than the call to be a minister. Many good words have been ruined by good people, like "pious" and "saint." But he should be both. Only the pure in heart see God. People sometimes enjoy a great sermon by a man whose life is suspect because of the brilliance of his mind and skill of his oratory, but this same man would have difficulty leading them in worship.

The pastor must practice the presence of God. His moments of meditation should be as many as possible, guarded from interruption, and as intense and devoted as a disciplined spirit can make them. He should read regularly the great prayers of the saints of all ages. This will not only deepen his spiritual life, feeding the wells of his soul, but will also enrich his vocabulary in public prayer and save him from cliché and repetition. We may not recognize each other's faces when we get to heaven but we will know our friends' prayers. I have a friend who enjoyed the phrase "when we shuffle off this mortal coil." I'm sure my soul will leap for joy when I hear that phrase in heaven some day. It'll be wonderful to "see" him again.

The leader in worship will also want to make a special effort at developing skills in the art of building worship services. Some of the books given in our bibliography will be of special help here. A work of art is "something out of this world" but it also demands certain techniques and skills to give it body and direction. The pastor will endeavor to understand how other people worship, including those not of his own denomination and not of the Christian faith. He will visit and observe and will make it a hobby to collect orders of service from which he can get new ideas of value. He will exchange worship folders with old friends and new ones in the ministry.

The Minister of Education

Much that has been said about the pastor will apply to the minister of education. He, too, must be God's man and must make both long-range and short-range preparation for leadership in worship. It is well to give him an opportunity to participate in the service in a significant way. He is also God's minister and will have a particular influence with a number of people. And Christian education and worship should be tied together in the minds and hearts of the people. Worship service No. 2 in the resource section is a good example of his worship ministry.

Enriching the Choir's Ministry

The minister of music, the organist, and the choirs of the church have a very vital part in leading the congregation in the worship of Almighty God. They definitely need a sense of mission about their work in harmony with the will of God and the spiritual tone of the church. They should be well trained and skilled, knowing the best music, and quite able to reproduce it. They should know well the people and their needs; what they like, and what they should be led to appreciate. The minister of music should continually make an effort to raise the level of musical appreciation of the congregation but not "fly too high" for their understanding. A balance is needed between what they want and what he thinks they should have. The minister of music must identify with the congregation and be a patient and loving teacher in their musical education. Of course, the first criterion for any selection is, Does it magnify Christ and stimulate divine worship?

The members of the choirs should be dedicated as well as capable people. Their attitude should be that of joyful reverence before, during, and after the service. Two or three members of a choir can hurt the spirit of worship by flirtation, whispering, and general indifference. Since they are often in front of the congregation and behind the preacher, to participate constructively and reverently during the sermon, for example, will take a special effort in discipline and concentration.

The music can pretty well make or break an evangelical service. Faithfulness, dependability, reverence, and quality of performance on the part of the minister of music, organist, and choir are a tremendous asset to any church. A wise pastor will express often his sincere gratitude and that of the people.

The Deacons and Worship

Deacons should be spiritual leaders of the congregation. In most cases, even though rotation in active service is practiced, they maintain continuity in spiritual leadership as pastors come and go. As is the case with the pastor, the congregation will seldom reach a higher level of spiritual experience than that of the deacons. They should be examples for other Christians to follow in life and in worship. As they engage in a pastoral ministry during the week they will be feeding the fires of warm, bright, happy worship on Sunday. The families with whom the deacon has prayed will very likely not only be in attendance at worship but will get a whole lot more out of it when they see him there. Another person with whom a deacon counseled about a problem will feel more at home in God's house because the deacon is there. The individual with whom another deacon talked about his need to make an open confession of faith in Jesus Christ will be much more apt to do just that when he sees and/or hears the deacon's confession of his own sins and his great need for forgiveness.

Some churches expect a deacon to be at church at every service, and the pastor is greatly helped by this kind of support. Such personal loyalty to the pastor is admirable. Such regularity at services is commendable. However, unless such faithfulness is centered on God and directly related to Christian ministry, as described in the preceding paragraph, it can become legalistic, burdensome, and a tinkling cymbal. But when it is so related the deacon feels the joy of spiritual service and fruitful endeavor, the worship service is greatly strengthened, and the angels of God rejoice.

The deacons can mean a very great deal to worship in many different ways. In some churches they meet with the pastor for prayer just before the beginning of the service. In most they receive the offerings of the people and present them to Almighty God in worship. The deacons may come into the service as a group, as the pastor and the choir enter, and sit at the front. This helps them lead the people in worship and serves as a further inspiration to the pastor in his role as leader. They are more readily available if called on for prayers of one kind or another. But it is well for them to be forewarned so they can make special preparation for this responsibility. They should speak loudly enough to be heard by all the congregation. In large churches a microphone should be used.

In many churches a deacon is selected for special honor and responsibility as "deacon of the week." His biography is often given in the church paper or in the worship folder. He usually is on the platform with the pastor as he engages in this ministry. If the church has divided the members of the congregation into groups, each one of which has been assigned to a deacon for pastoral ministry, those members who are the responsibility of the "deacon of the week" could be given recognition in some appropriate way.

There are advantages and disadvantages in everything this side of heaven. One disadvantage of much that has been suggested above is that the deacon never gets to worship with his family. This is not good, especially if the spouse is in the choir or otherwise engaged and children are involved. Witness in worship is greatly served as people gather together as families to sing God's praise.

Spiritual Women

The churches of the New Testament were greatly blessed by good and faithful women. Widows devoted to the Lord's work had a special place. God apparently expects the men to bear the major responsibility of leadership in service and worship in the churches but most congregations would be very weak without the ladies, and some would likely die. Women who are given to prayer, to Bible study, to the progress of God's kingdom in their interest in persons, in missions, and community service are of inestimable value to the church and her worship. Many of them are capable and devoted leaders of the church and community. They are homemakers, Christian educators, businesswomen, schoolteachers, social service counselors and other vocations. The presence of an inner circle of dedicated, spiritual women can elevate the tone of any service of worship.

Ushers and Greeters

The ushers and greeters have the responsibility and privilege of being hosts to the congregation. Like any host or hostess they can set the tone of the whole service. They greet the people in the name of God and that particular church of the Lord Jesus Christ. They measure their graciousness by the grace of our Lord. The outcast will receive special attention but not condescension. He is apt to be very sensitive and could be lost by a thoughtless word or act. On the other hand, the visitor could be discourteous, perhaps failing to follow the leadership of the usher and make him feel foolish. The host will take it in good spirit, remembering the infinitely greater rejection suffered by his Lord.

Every congregation will make an effort to be a blessing to visitors in a way that does not embarrass people and seems appropriate to the church. Except in very unusual circumstances the leader in worship will avoid a hilarious, civic-club type welcome, telling a joke about this locality or that. His welcome and that of the ushers will be relaxed and friendly, but one that remembers that the purpose of the occasion is to worship Almighty God. Most churches give the visitors an opportunity to register their presence on a card or in a book. This should be followed by a cordial letter and, where possible, a visit from the pastor and/or a deacon. The visit will endeavor to meet the particular need of persons and minister to their welfare.

Children and Youth

Happy and blessed is the congregation that has a group of children and youth who know how to worship God. They should be taught the best hymns. They can learn to love these even more than those of less permanent value, beloved by their parents. Of course they will have some of their own which will be only a passing fancy.

Their Christian education should make the most of their sense of wonder, appreciation for mystery, and their love of the beautiful. They should be taught early about the love of God and led to experience it in a vital way, each for himself. When they are capable of understanding a meaningful relationship to Jesus

Christ, they will be given the opportunity to commit their lives to him. They will be encouraged to grow in spiritual development and independence and should be given an opportunity for leadership in worship in their own group at an early age. They will probably find their first opportunity for leading the whole congregation in worship as they sing in a choir.

Informing the Congregation

When we think of the word "inform," we usually have the idea of education and information. But, according to Webster the word primarily means to "give form or character to," and to "inspire" and "to animate." The congregation does have need for teaching about worship. This is certainly one of the purposes of this book—to help leaders inspire and teach worshiping congregations. But worship, like religion is rather "caught" than "taught."

The people can be inspired to worship God at a higher level of Christian experience by sermons preached on the subject. The several qualities of a good worship service could be discussed with them. This could be done on Sunday morning, or evening, or at the midweek service. When the order of service is to be changed substantially, they should be told of it by appropriate means and the main reasons for the change discussed. Printed worship folders are particularly helpful and are now used by most churches.

The Worship Committee

Many congregations are finding it helpful to have a worship committee representative of the important groups discussed above. The personnel of the committee would include the pastor, minister of music, organist, choir director, minister of education, a deacon, the chairman of the ushers, a woman, and a young person deeply interested in worship.

This committee will endeavor to find out from the congregation just what they want in worship services. This should grow out of the church's study of itself and its role in God's kingdom. This is a part of the administrative and programmatic process of the congregation. The worship committee will continually remind the church council and other leaders, as well as the whole congregation, that the church must know God and herself in worship before she can expect to do anything else as it should be done. The worship life of the church will be determined by the people who make up the congregation. Their tradition, habits, and customs, and their view of what a church is supposed to be and do will lead to their kind of worship.

In the effort of the church to find herself there should be a thorough study of New Testament churches and how they worshiped. The tradition of the denomination and of that local church will be examined. The present needs of the congregation and the people of the community will be sympathetically surveyed. It would be well for the worship committee to follow this up in every detail with the question, What does this mean for our worship today?

The pastor and minister of music could collect worship folders of all different types for examination by the committee. After several sessions of hard study, the committee should report to the church, indicating some ways in which the services of worship could be enriched for the glory of God and the spiritual uplift of the people. It would be wise, of course, to indicate to the congregation that the committee is the servant of the church and does not expect to move faster than the main body of the congregation desires.

Planning Worship Services

We could have started this chapter at this point. Most pastors and church staffs have made an effort at reformation in worship practices without involving the congregation and other groups mentioned above. Of course it can be done this way and often has to be done in this manner for any one of a number of reasons. But it should be apparent to the reader that the team of planners is much better prepared for its work if it carries on its task with the kind of spiritual and intelligent support which can and will be given by people who are trained and informed.

The worship committee should do some long-range planning in harmony with that done by the congregation under the leadership of the church council or similar group. At least one year's program should be outlined, keeping in mind the several emphases of the church, the denomination, and the Christian year. But the week by week arranging of the orders of service will be done by persons more directly responsible for leadership in worship. This team will be composed of the pastor, the minister of music, the organist, the minister of education with the addition of anyone else this group needs for doing the work. Perhaps this person last named will change with recurring emphases, or the use of different choirs, etc. Of course not all churches will have this many people on the team. Some will have a few more. In the majority of churches the minister and the choir director will be the team.

The pastor will serve as captain. The equipment will include hymnals, a list of special music ready or nearly ready for singing, instrumental music available for use, the Holy Bible, resources for worship services published in books of compilations, ministers' manuals like Segler's *The Broadman Minister's Manual,* *The Book of Common Prayer,* books of religious poems, a file of worship folders used by the congregation in the past, and a collection of worship folders from other churches.

The pastor will remind the group of the emphasis for that period in the life of the church, and especially that of the coming Sunday. If he has not already done so, he will share his sermon topic with the group, give them some idea of what he means by it, and what he thinks the aim or purpose of the service should be.

For purposes of this discussion let us assume that the planning team intends to follow the order designated No. 1 in the "resource section" at the back of this book. This particular service was obtained from the First Baptist Church of Seattle, Washington, when the author worshiped with that congregation several years ago. In his opinion it is still an excellent order and has been updated. It is particularly helpful in teaching a congregation just what they are doing when they take part in a service. Many people have followed a certain habit since before they can remember and have little idea of what is going on. The outline of this service stands out bold and clear. There can be no mistake as to what each part is designed to help people do in worship. For a person who is of long experience and quite skilled in worship this order might seem mechanical. But we're not concerned about him at the moment. We'll try to have something helpful for him later.

(May we suggest that the reader get a couple of bookmarks and use them for holding places as we refer back and forth between the text and the resource section.)

We have used this order of service on several occasions and it has been a great spiritual blessing to many people. The two paragraphs at the top are both used as preparation for worship, although one is mainly a word of welcome. The first paragraph may be changed once a month. It is a call to worship that is general in nature. The second paragraph should be changed every Sunday in keeping with the theme for the day. The pastor would probably have the responsibility for selecting these quotations, or writing something original.

The people responsible for the music will make suggestions of selections they think are appropriate. The organ prelude or "musical meditation" in order No. 1 is particularly appropriate to the theme and is a beautiful and very worshipful piece of music of lasting value. Perhaps a more appropriate hymn would be "Holy, Holy, Holy" but the one selected is excellent as an invocation hymn next to the prayer of invocation.

The pastor will help with the decision as to the hymns to be sung especially the one used for invitation. Often he tends to be reluctant to try anything new, and the minister of music is likely to be an innovator. They need to balance each other.

The congregation more easily accepts new words than new tunes. By checking the names of familiar and beloved tunes in the index of the hymnal the team will often come across a new hymn of words to the old tune, which words are quite appropriate to the theme of the day. The hymn "Just As I Am," for example, is perhaps the greatest invitational hymn of all time. But even it can be overdone. "God Calling Yet! Shall I Not Hear?" has excellent appeal in new words to that popular tune.

The placement of the special music in the serivce is very important. Sometimes an anthem is a prayer and should go near one. Sometimes it can be more appropriately used near the sermon. It is well for the pastor to know what the choral benediction will be so he will not give it first and embarrass the choir.

If one or more laymen are to be used in the service for the reading of the Scripture or one or more of the prayers they should be agreed upon by the planners. Responsibility should be taken for enlisting their services and for reporting their assent to the person who will prepare the service for printing.

The planning team may take a few minutes to look ahead two or more Sundays to see what emphases are in the offing. The theme for next Sunday, at least, should be agreed upon. It would help the minister of music, especially if he could know the minister's sermons for several weeks ahead. Some anthems take many hours of work in preparation.

The group responsible for weekly planning will confer with the worship committee about once a month and will endeavor to learn from them and from the congregation any suggestions they may have as to the strengths and weaknesses of the services.

3

Planning Special Worship Services

The days of a man's life are not democratic. There are high and holy days, days that are vital and strategic. Birth and death, regeneration and baptism, marriage and parenthood, calling to service and commitment to vocation, falling into sin and restoration through forgiveness, leaving the fellowship and rejoining it in the Lord's Supper make for memorable days that call for special celebration in worship.

The Importance of Baptism

The baptism of Jesus was the beginning of the gospel according to the New Testament. One of the qualifications of an apostle was that he was a witness of Jesus' baptism. Jesus spoke often of his own baptism and apparently related it to his crucifixion and his divine mission of salvation for men.

Biblical scholars seldom make dogmatic statements about New Testament practice, even though they may about doctrine. An outstanding group of them declared: "It is beyond dispute that in no Church body does baptism have the decisive significance which the witness of the New Testament ascribes to it."[1] In other words, Christians today just do not take baptism as seriously as New Testament Christians did. Baptism does not mean as much to us now as it did to them then.

Perhaps we have been so busy arguing about the mode (immersion) that we have failed to look for the meaning. And maybe we have been so afraid of sacramentalism that we have been unwilling to let ourselves go in the search for meaning. We might find more than we could stand. The argument for immersion has been largely won. Most scholars agree that it was the New Testament way. Believer's baptism is vital for Christian faith and practice. It is basic to the freedom of religion, and

31

helps support the other freedoms of our civilization: citizenship, press, vocation, etc.

There is a wealth of material on baptism in the New Testament, much more than on the Lord's Supper, for example. It was and is the gospel in action. There is no Christian doctrine but finds expression in baptism. We owe it to ourselves as Christians and as responsible Christian teachers of others to make a serious study of the New Testament message on this very vital subject. Of course every study of the Bible will bring many blessings but a search for new truth on this subject will deepen and enrich one's Christian faith immeasurably. George R. Beasley-Murray's *Baptism in the New Testament* is probably the greatest book in the field. B. F. Smith's *Christian Baptism* (Broadman Press) is an outstanding work and helpful in understanding the different options in baptismal practice. See other books on baptism in the annotated bibliography in the resource section.

A service of worship means as much to us as we are prepared for it to mean, no more, no less. Some churches will fight you over the mode, the administrator, and the absolute necessity of baptism for church membership. Then they'll have it before a service begins, or after it ends, and with little preparation of candidate or church for it. George W. Truett often used the unusual word *expectancy*. Too many people, candidates, congregations, and even pastors have no expectancy about baptism. They're looking for nothing to happen and the Holy Spirit doesn't disappoint or surprise them. They are satisfied about two things. It was commanded by our Lord. They have obeyed his commandment. They expect to use it as a witness, and they have witnessed.

Have Baptists made baptism too much of an individual matter for the candidate? The most important person at a baptismal service is Jesus Christ. In baptism it is also important to emphasize the church, the baptizing church, the ongoing, past, present, future, eternal church. We should also expect the Holy Spirit to be present. Apollos had experienced John's baptism. It was all right in mode but was inadequate without the Spirit.

If baptism meant more to us, at least three good fruits would

result. First, there would be less "dip them and drop them."
Second, the churches would be strengthened spiritually as they
felt the Spirit's power in baptism and took more responsibility for
the new candidates. Third, and probably most important, it
would make for more ethical living on a higher moral plane.
For example, what is the main point Paul is making in the
reference to baptism in Romans 6:1-4? Most of us have used
it as an argument for immersion as the only proper mode of
baptism. That's all right. But Paul had something else in mind:
"When we were baptized into union with Christ Jesus, we were
baptized into union with his death. By our baptism, then, we
were buried with him and shared his death, in order that, just
as Christ was raised from death by the glorious power of the
Father, so also we might live a new life" (v.3). In baptism
we are reminded that the old sinful man is dead, and the new
raised-up person, that we are, has no business giving way to
sinful temptations.

But this is not a book on the meaning of baptism. Our apolo-
gies for discussing it at length. But it is our conviction that if
our baptismal services are going to be services of worship we
must begin with a deep appreciation and full understanding of
what we are doing.

Improving the Baptismal Service

The first thing we can do to help the baptism mean more
to the church, the candidates, and their families is to give it a
service of its own. Baptism, for almost everyone, happens just
once in a lifetime. It is unique, the only experience of its kind.
It is a fateful step. We will never forget it. The Holy Spirit
sometimes comes in a wonderful way at baptism. We should
look for him and pray for his blessing. The baptism of one's
child, or husband, or wife is something extra special. We've
prayed for it, longed for it, anticipated it, and now here is the
moment of God's grace. And what about the church into which
the candidates will come? Is there not a special concern and
an awesome responsibility? For all these reasons and others baptism is worthy of a service set aside just for this particular occasion.

We should make every effort to magnify baptism and make it more meaningful to all by selecting appropriate hymns. Unfortunately, there are very few baptismal hymns available. Perhaps the one known best by our people is the one written to the tune of a drinking song. Some in the hymnbooks need to be learned. Others should be written. A great service could be rendered here and eternal gratitude obtained. See No. 3 in the resource section for one worthy effort.

The Scripture selections should be carefully made and a baptismal sermon preached. The pastor should take the opportunity to instruct and inspire the people with regard to this great ordinance. As indicated above there is a multitude of good texts on the subject. The candidates particularly will be attentive to new truth from God's Word. Every Christian will relive his own baptism much as each married person is reminded of his own vows when he attends a wedding.

It is important to emphasize the solemn commitment of the candidate to Christ, and also the responsibility of the church. See Nos. 4, 5, and 6 in the resource section. Apparently all the candidates were children in No. 5.

In *The Broadman Minister's Manual* Segler gives detailed instructions in an excellent way on the mechanics of baptizing. We would also stress the importance of making the ordinance as personal as possible. The candidate's name should be used in the pronouncement or just before it. It is good to ask some question along this line: "Do you take Jesus Christ as your personal Savior and the Lord of your life" When the candidate gives the affirmative answer the baptism follows.

Some early Baptists in England and also in this country followed baptism with the laying on of hands. The custom is presently followed by Danish Baptists. The order goes like this. When the candidate has dressed following his baptism, he comes into the sanctuary. The minister then reads appropriate Scripture and gives the candidate the right hand of fellowship. While the candidate is kneeling and the congregation is standing, the pastor lays his hand upon the head of the candidate and dedicates him to the care of God and to the confirmation of the Holy Spirit. It is a free prayer, not a formal one. Participation of the new member in the Lord's Supper follows.

The Baptismal Setting

Everything possible should be done to make the setting for worship at the baptismal service as beautiful and as reverent as possible. Some churches will have electric devices like rheostats, special lighting, a beautiful baptistry and elaborate robes. Others will use surplices from the choir, candles, and other means to make the service different and impressive, yet dignified and reverent. A good imagination can improve a poor situation, but it is better to do too little than too much and overshadow the service itself.

The Lord's Supper

Baptism is once for all, the Lord's Supper is recurrent. The Supper is the gospel in action, too. It is a proclamation of a past act—the sacrifice of the Lord for our salvation—in faith and thanksgiving. It is the pronouncement of a present experience, fellowship with and love for Christ and with other Christians. It is a prophecy of a future event—eating the Supper with Jesus in the heavenly Kingdom.

Underhill declares that the foundations of Christian worship are the Word and the Eucharist, the Bible and the Lord's Supper, the sermon and Communion. In the Middle Ages the Roman Catholic emphasized the Mass and virtually forgot the sermon. Many Baptists have often neglected the Supper but felt they could not worship without the sermon. One is the gospel in word, the other the gospel in action. The New Testament churches seem to have used both pillars of worship very frequently. Some Christians today insist that each service should have the Supper or anticipate it—communion or ante-communion.

The New Testament gives few directions about how to observe the Supper. Unworthy celebration is condemned in 1 Corinthians 11:20-22 and 27-34. The so-called "Words of Institution" are found in 1 Corinthians 11:23-26. The Synoptic Gospels give an account of the institution by our Lord. But there is no indication here or in any later reference to its observance by the early churches as to any fixed time for it, or about frequency required, or any stated order of worship.

Guidelines for Observance

We do have enough information to give us some guidelines. To be true to the New Testament and to the gospel the observance should keep these things in mind: (1) it is a fellowship meal instituted by our Lord to remind us of his sacrifice for our salvation; (2) the furniture holding the elements should be considered a family table and never an altar; (3) the leader in worship may be anyone so designated by the congregation but is usually the pastor; (4) the leader should not do anything that would make him a priest superior to his people, e.g., acting like a priest in turning his back to the people and pleading for his people before an altar; (5) as much participation of deacons as possible and also of choir and congregation should be planned; (6) magical implications in connection with the blessing of the bread and the cup should be avoided, the praise of God, gratitude to him and to Jesus Christ should dominate such prayers; (7) the service should be reverent, full of joy and thanksgiving, not somber and sad; (8) the presence of Christ should be the pervading spirit of the service; (9) food for the soul is spiritual food, spiritually sought, spiritually given, and spiritually received, (no magical change of the physical into the spiritual); (10) the people should be led from confession of sin to a sense of forgiveness of sin, and then to rededication of life and work.

Some Sample Services

The worship service for the Lord's Supper should be planned with these purposes in mind. Unless a definite effort is made in a direction which the Holy Spirit can use, it will become a meaningless ritual. Baptists have had a tendency to neglect the observance and, in fear of sacramentalism, to make it perfunctory. Some have thought of it as something that must be done because our Lord commanded it. They have tacked it on the end of what they considered a more important service. If this has been the history of your church. a special effort in planning a very meaningful service must be made. Perhaps service No. 7 to be found in the research section is especially designed to meet this need. It is not too formal, uses familiar hymns, and has plenty of opportunity for congregational participation. It also fosters a relaxed mood of meditation and contemplation.

Let's look at service No. 7. It begins with a prayer to be used in preparation for worship. When a person enters the house of the Lord he should go quietly to his seat and bow his head, praying for the service, for the leaders in worship, for the congregation and for himself. The call to worship is antiphonal, the minister reading a bit of Scripture and the choir responding with another in song; about four or five responses apiece. The Gloria Patri is a very ancient doxology and should be sung with adoration and joy. The prayer of invocation and the Lord's Prayer follow.

Another feature of service No. 7 is the setting apart of the "service of giving." Before the dawn of history the making of a sacrificial offering was the climax of man's worship. The Doxology is our "song of the Lord." The sermon should be one that does everything possible to prepare people and pastor for the Lord's Supper. It should be shorter than usual so everyone will be relaxed about the time. Clock-watching is an unfortunate tension of our time.

During the hymn of fellowship the minister will come to the table, and the chairman of the diaconate will join him there. If there is a cloth over the elements it will be removed at this point. The minister will quote, or give in his own way the "words of institution" (1 Cor. 11:23-26) and will lead the people naturally and yet reverently into the prayers. If they are open to the Spirit and are thinking about their sins and their Lord's suffering, they will be driven to confession and a cry for forgiveness and blessing.

The pastor will say a few words about the bread, will break it, and with the help of the chairman of the diaconate give it to the deacons. The organist will play appropriate music quietly meanwhile, and the pastor and people will pray and meditate silently as the Lord leads them to do so. The "hymn of trust" may be sung as the deacons return, if desired by the team planning the service. In this case the deacons will wait at the back of the sanctuary until the organist plays a brief introduction to the hymn. She will be watching them as they serve the people and will not start the introduction until all are ready. The choir will lead the congregation in the singing, seated. The pastor should not stand at the beginning of the hymn. To do so might trigger the habit of the people to stand at the start of a hymn and this would lead to confusion and break the spirit of the moment. Some churches prefer to wait until the deacons have returned and they and pastor have been served for the hymn to be sung. Again the organist will give the cue.

The sharing of the cup follows in similar fashion. Perhaps, when this order is first used, the pastor at the end of his sentences about the cup could ask the people to keep the cups in hand until after the prayer of dedication. Too often there is distracting clatter and confusion at the very moment when the climax of the service is reached. A sincere desire for rededication should overflow each Christian's heart.

Emphasizing the Gospel in Action

One of the oldest Baptist churches in the world is New Road Baptist Church of Oxford, England. Rev. Eric Sharpe, an outstanding leader in a revival of interest in worship, prepared the order of service numbered 8 in the resource section. His purpose was twofold. He wished to help his people understand the service better and so get more spiritual benefit. He wanted also to emphasize the *action,* as Jesus apparently did, in relating the memorial supper to his death on the cross. You will note that the order of service is on the left and a running comment on the action is on the right. We will discuss some of the peculiarities of the service in Chapter 6, but the special features relating to the Supper will be noted here.

Among the meaningful points brought out is the emphasis upon participation in the making of the offering. Many people have stood when the offering is being presented for years without knowing why. Identification of the giver with the gift is extremely important for meaningful worship. The offering of the bread and the wine with the money comes from New Testament times. Then the people brought food and clothing for the poor, and what little money they had, and offered it all to God for his glory and benefit of his people. The leader in worship then took some of the bread and wine given and used it in the service of the Supper.

Giving everyone the opportunity to stay or leave is interesting. Here is open communion, but with emphasis upon individual choice. In this particular church very few, if any, left. But in other British Baptist churches visited by this writer a large part of the congregation departed, including some members of the church. In one church the pastor went to the door and told the people good-by. After some confusion, and the people remaining had rearranged themselves for better serving, the Supper was begun.

In service No. 8 the three actions of Jesus are emphasized: giving thanks, breaking the bread and giving it, pouring the wine and giving it. You will note one very fine idea. The bread was received and eaten individually. The wine was held and all drank together. "Thus we signify both the individual and corporate nature of our Communion" says the pastor.

Action and Meditation at the Table

Service No. 9 constitutes an excellent example of planning by the leaders in worship. Every detail was carefully thought out. The skills of several people were enlisted. The result is a very worshipful service. It may seem formal to some people but there is certainly nothing mysterious about it and one could feel at home with the hymns, anthem, and solo. It excels in the call to participation. It moves rapidly without a dull moment. Perhaps the choir does too much and the people should do more. This would be put in better balance if the congregation joined the choir in singing the three hymns connected with the Supper itself.

Perhaps an unusual feature of No. 9 is found in the three meditations given. They were delivered as the minister stood at the table. Each one made an appropriate point and was addressed directly to each person in the congregation. Stepping out from behind the pulpit and coming down and speaking to the people on their level has real psychological advantages.

The service also made much of the gospel in action. A loaf of bread was broken before the people. A pitcher of grape juice was poured out into a large cup before their eyes. The broken body and the spilt blood were better visualized and understood. You will also note that "delivery" is emphasized in each case.

Service No. 10 found in the resource section is more in line with usual practice in evangelical churches. It excels in continually keeping before the minds of people the different ways in which they are worshiping. It also features movement and progress and goes purposely from where the people are, needing preparation, step by step to higher and higher ground until the peak is reached in the celebration of the Supper.

Service No. 11 is an example of how the two ordinances may be tied together in one very meaningful service. There are sound theological foundations for this and it is especially valuable to those persons who have just been baptized. There are obvious problems involved. The planning group will need to take special care in arranging such a service.

Using Calendars in Planning

The committee on worship and the planning team will keep in mind three calendars which greatly influence the life of the church. The first is the calendar of the community, that of the secular year. The dates of the public school should be known. The people live in this world and it cannot be ignored. To plan a series of revival services at the time of the district basketball tournament is to court disaster. It is not a question of arguing about priorities. There's a time for everything under the sun and church leaders are wise when they work positively and cheerfully with the community. The community will usually then work with the church.

The second calendar influencing planning is that of the denomination. Missions, education, the several benevolent and charitable institutions, and the different organizations of the church must be taken into account in making plans. Most of them will furnish appropriate material for building appropriate services of worship which emphasize their needs.

The third calendar is that of the Christian year. While that of the denomination is a worthy and necessary one of promotion, this is one of devotion. Most Christians around the world use it and it has remained much the same for centuries. It features events in the life of Jesus and of the early church. In this way what Christ did for us in his life and death come alive for us in meaningful personal experiences. One of its greatest values is that it gives the congregation a balanced spiritual diet for the year. Most pastors are prone to emphasize one aspect of Christian truth and neglect others. He can still ride his hobby horse but not as comfortably when he pays at least some attention to the Christian year.

Using the Christian Year in Planning

Of course the three calendars mentioned above will be used extensively by the church council or similar planning group. The worship committee and members of the worship planning team will have their say when decisions are made in the council. When those plans have been adopted by the church, the worship committee and the planning team will work accordingly. Perhaps the church would not want to have anything to do with the Christian year. They would still be Christians, of course, but would be refusing some of the riches of their inheritance. And it would be almost impossible to ignore Christmas and Easter. And how could they enjoy poverty in leaving out Pentecost? By doing as they please, of course.

The Christian year begins with Advent, the first coming of Jesus Christ. It starts four Sundays before Christmas. It is the best answer to the commercialization of the season. It helps prepare the hearts and lives of the people for the coming of the Christ "who is newly born, and newly dear" every year. Every Christian needs a fresh experience of this Christ. He has a choice between bedlam and Bethlehem at a very busy time. The derivation of the word "bedlam" will illustrate the point. It comes from an old mental hospital in London which was called Bethlehem. The English have a way of running their syllables together. When a visitor passing by the hospital would ask about all the noise and confusion the reply was, "O that's just Bethlem." And so the word bedlam was brought to birth.

Another important season of the Christian year is that of Lent. No. 12 in the resource section is a short service used in a school chapel on Ash Wednesday. It is self-explanatory. It could be adapted for use at prayer meeting on that particular Wednesday night. With more time available a sermon on self-examination and repentance would be quite in order.

The eight days ending in Easter constitute Holy Week. It begins with Palm Sunday and its perennial question, Will you crown or crucify Jesus Christ? There is a wealth of material in the Bible and plenty of music upon which the planning team may draw in building a worship service for this day.

Thursday night before Easter is the one on which our Lord instituted the Lord's Supper. The annual observance of this significant event can be a tremendous blessing to the people and make every Lord's Supper service more meaningful. The planning team can build a worship service which emphasizes the trials of Jesus on Monday, the day of confrontation in the Temple, and Tuesday, the long day of controversy with differing groups of his enemies. Wednesday was apparently a day of physical rest and spiritual strengthening in Bethany.

Several sources are listed in the bibliography which will be of great help to the planning team in building worship services during the Christian year. Most of them are arranged according to the Christian calendar, and have selections for every part of the service from the call to worship to the benediction. Excellent quotations from religious classics which may be used for paragraphs in preparation for worship are available, as are poems, and, of course, Scripture selections.

Easter Sunday means much more to the Christian when he has meditated seriously and devotedly upon the suffering and death of his Lord. All through the darkness of late Thursday and very early Friday Jesus went through many trials, literally and figuratively. Good Friday, or Black Friday, was the day of his crucifixion. A Good Friday service has been held throughout

Christendom for centuries. Worship service No. 13 features the seven words from the cross. Countless sermons have been preached on each one of them. Apparently only three people carried the whole burden of responsibility in this service. Usually several ministers and many singers lead the Good Friday service as churches of the community come together for it. Again, there is plenty of material available in books listed in the bibliography and elsewhere.

NOTES

1. World Council of Churches Commission on Faith and Order, *One Lord, One Baptism,* p. 70.

4

Planning Other Special Services

Services of worship in the churches change with changing customs and living habits of the people. Seventy-five years ago the evening hour was better attended than the morning. About fifty years earlier night after night meetings were originated in the fervor of the revival movement. That's why they were called "protracted" meetings. Radio, TV, and the family car have almost eliminated the Sunday evening service in many churches. The "prayer meeting fraternity" has been reduced to a mere handful in most places and entirely lost in others. What can we do about these losses?

We certainly should not waste any time in a mournful dirge. We should also remember that we are more interested in God and in people than we are in propping up an organization or sacred custom. We must go back to our original questions: What are we as church, under God, supposed to be and do? What do the people of the church and community really need? How best can we meet these needs? The answers to these questions may indicate that we must try harder and get new ideas in using the customary hours of worship. It may also mean that we must ask the Holy Spirit to lead us to entirely new times of meeting and to new methods. He has done this many times in the past. With the exception of the Sunday morning service practically every organization and meeting time for worship now used by evangelical Christians is less than two hundred years old. Today our people have more leisure time than ever before and undoubtedly a greater need for God than ever. Surely the Lord is expecting us to increase the number and greatly improve the quality of our experiences of worship.

In many churches the evening service is almost a copy of that of the morning. And one half to three fourths of the people present were there that morning. An entirely different kind of service would stimulate their spiritual taste buds and would probably attract some people who are not interested in a traditional service. Item No. 14 in the resource section gives an example of a simple play of long vintage and deep meaning. It also has an announcement of "Church Night" on Wednesday evening. This plan for the midweek has been very successful in many churches. Now some congregations are reversing the plan with Sunday evening largely one of interest groups of many kinds for all ages and Wednesday night with a vesper service.

The worship committee and the planning team, the point is, will endeavor to meet the needs of the people in ways in which they can get their support. It should be kept in mind also that there are emphases in the denominational calendar and that of the Christian year which call for many Sunday and Wednesday evenings. In addition, there will be special services connected with the life of the local church which often can better be held on Sunday or Wednesday evening. These include the ordination of deacons (service No. 15), ordination of a minister (item 16) or a chain of praying persons in preparation for a revival (No. 17). The Lord's Supper should be observed in the evening at least once a year. There are people who can't come to church on Sunday morning.

Services of dedication of buildings or equipment are usually held on Sunday mornings or afternoons. The planning committee will want to do its best. This will be the only service of its kind, most likely, for a generation in that church. Sometimes very elaborate orders of worship are outlined and beautiful and distinctive folders are printed. Because of lack of space we are offering a simple service in item No. 18.

More and more Christian young people are dissatisfied with pagan weddings and are planning worship services of which the marriage ceremony is a part. Often they make out their own service but the planning team should help as needed. Of course the minister must be consulted and his approval given. Service No. 19 is an excellent example of such a service. It has deep spiritual overtones. It is biblical and involves the congregation in affirmation and covenant. In a note to guests the persons planning the service wrote: "In a service of worship celebrating a marriage, preeminently, we celebrate the goodness of God who is with us and promises to be with us always. Thus marriage is a sacrament of the Christian community; and its celebration is joyous and thankful worship of God, our confidence and our hope."

Devotional services for retreats should be carefully planned with the purpose of the meeting and special needs and tastes kept in mind. Such occasions lend themselves to more experimentation and also to more ritual. There is a wide latitude of choice, therefore, and the most should be made of it. These groups are by the nature of the situation more open to the leadership of the Spirit into new paths. That's one of the main values of a retreat. Service No. 20 makes excellent use of the Scriptures, putting them in the center and using them for a direct appeal to the heart of the worshiper. Resources from treasuries of Christian history which have stood the test of time and blessed many generations of Christians are featured. To the uninitiated the readings may seem too long. Many people are not used to giving that much attention in their devotions, or working that hard for the Lord in worship. But attention, concentration, contemplation, and meditation are the life and substance of worship. By changing only a few words in the text the service may be used in the evening. (A portion of No. 20 is shown.)

The prayer our Lord gave to his disciples as a model of praise and petition may be used as the inspiration of a morning meditation for individual or corporate devotions. An example is given as item No. 21.

New Departures in Worship Planning

We said earlier that we are experiencing today a veritable revolution in worship planning and practice as great as and perhaps more radical than that of the Reformation. This time the Roman Catholic Church is a part of the change rather than reacting more conservatively against it. The Reformers did make fundamental changes. They abolished the priesthood. They restored preaching to a prominent place in the worship service. They restored the vernacular as the language of worship. Congregational participation was greatly increased and extemporaneous prayer encouraged. Prayers for and to or through the saints were forbidden. The altars were turned into tables, and the repeated sacrifice of our Lord in the Mass was vigorously rejected. In general, they aimed at restoring the spirit and much of the practice of New Testament worship. Of course, there were great differences between them. Luther was probably the most conservative and the Anabaptists the most radical.

But in the great majority of the churches of the reformers there was still much form and considerable ritual. In appearance much was as it was before. There was considerable distinction between minister and laymen. Dignity in dress and demeanor prevailed. The people were still the audience and the spectators seated in rows as in a theatre watching a performance.

A new reformation is in the wind today. It's too early yet to tell whether or not it is another Reformation bringing an upsurge of the human spirit lifted by the Spirit of God. Several years ago G. K. Chesterton and a friend were standing on a street corner listening to a meeting of the Salvation Army. As the last strains of the brass band were ended, Chesterson's friend remarked somewhat contemptuously, "I don't like that kind of stuff," to which he received the answer, "No, but supposing God does!" We are experiencing the same question today.

There are really two mainstreams of change in worship practices calling for our attention now. And they are at opposite ends of the spectrum. The more conservative movement is about fifty years old. Its main desire has been to enrich and deepen our religious experience in corporate worship by reclaiming from our Christian heritage all that is good and true and beautiful so that our religious life may be strengthened and deepened to the glory of God. We could call this the priestly thrust. It has flowed from two sources: a tremendous increase in interest in biblical theology, and the reexamination by each denomination of its conception of the church as stimulated by the ecumenical movement. These fountains have meant very much to the life of the churches. Without these waters many of them would have withered and died and all the churches have been blessed by them. You will see evidences of this revival of interest in worship of the more traditional sort in the bibliography given in this volume. British Baptists have been particularly strong in this movement. This book is undoubtedly indebted to it.

The other mainstream of change in worship in our time has been of a rebellious sort. It has the spirit of rejection of the church as an institution. Some of its adherents have given up on the church. All of them like to wake people up if not shock them in their lethargy. Theirs is the spirit of the prophet who is impatient with feast days and pomp and ceremony and speaks often of hypocrisy. There is a sense of depression in the examination of one's own sins and those of the society of which he is a part. There is an emphasis upon love and brotherhood, beauty and goodness, the earth and earthly things. Rejecting order in worship and in about everything else, this movement inevitably comes up with its own order. It rejoices in song and drama and the ecstasy of celebration. Above all it wants to be relevant and out where the action is. It is a fast-growing cult and has developed its own literature, music, and life-style.

Most of the followers of this new left in worship practices are young people, and some of them look and act like "hippies." It is shocking to the uninitiated to see bare feet, ragged clothes, miniskirts, stringy hair, and lounging "bodes" in all sorts of positions around the room. Sometimes fast-flickering and blinding lights, and all kinds of weird sound effects are used. The music is often personal and sentimental, and at times beautiful and idealistic. It usually has plenty of rhythm. The leaders of the Reformation would be astounded by such antics in the name of worship.

The young people are especially interested in honesty about the world and themselves. And they are anxious to break down walls between people, especially any barrier that keeps them from getting in the act or hinders communication. For example, a group illustrating modern drama began with each person on stage going along the footlights rubbing his hands and pushing against what they later declared to be an invisible wall of glass between them and the audience. They then began to heckle the audience into participation in the "act" and when things began to go well they shouted "The wall is down!"

In one prayer service everyone present was asked to write

on a card anything that was "bugging him," or any desire he may have for a friend to forgive him, or a description of a situation which he was finding difficult. All "requests" were written anonymously. The cards were put on a wire at the front of the room with clothespins. After some glad-handing the group settled down and the problems were read out one at a time. A hymn, a prayer, or a testimony was offered by anyone who felt led to respond to that particular problem which was apparently upon the hearts of all present and a real desire to help was manifest.

Of course there are all kinds of people interested in this new "priesthood of all believers." The old as well as young find warmth and release in it. The Roman Catholics, perhaps made hungrier than most groups by centuries of restrictions, are leaders in the movement. We attended an interfaith meeting of professors of Christian education. One period of worship was led by the Catholics. The singing was led by a nun in modern, though quite modest, dress. Our singing was accompanied by a couple, man and wife, playing guitars. The music was typical of the new religion, excellent rhythm with some good lyrics of praise of Jesus Christ. A priest led in a free prayer using "you" instead of "thee" and "thou" in addressing God. It seemed to us that the Lord's blessing was upon this service.

Like any revolutionary movement there are excesses. And there are always people who will endeavor to make a profit in money or personal esteem. How much of it is a passing fad we do not know. We are sure that what is of God will remain, and that which is not will soon be forgotten. Of course, there is a mixture of good and bad in almost everything. For example, the musical, *Jesus Christ, Superstar* has some good parts. But it cannot be called Christian as a whole because it stops short of the resurrection, the central doctrine of our faith. It must have been written by pagans who see life as a heroic adventure but basically without hope. The most "super" thing Jesus did was to overcome death, our greatest enemy, and to make eternal life available for us all.

We can learn a very great deal from this new movement. It has something to say to us that is true to God and to the Bible that we have forgotten and fail to practice. It is right in declaring that our God is a God of action. It is true that he has used many media in his communication of himself to us, not just words. It is also true that many people prefer to worship God in small groups in informal settings like a social hall, recreation room, dining area around tables, and the relaxed atmosphere of a living room or den. So we must take a pluralistic approach to worship and not try to crowd all of our people into a single box at eleven o'clock on Sunday morning. "Box" is a harsh word, but our beautiful sanctuaries feel like that to some people who are pressed into a pew and given little opportunity to witness to their faith.

So our worship committee and planning team must encourage variety in kinds of worship in a variety of places at a number of different times according to the needs and desires of the people. Again we return to the fundamental question each church must ask herself, What kind of church does God want us to be and what kind are we willing to be today? Some will answer this question one way and some another. This is not just true of worship, but also of evangelism, and of missions, and of community service. It would be unfortunate if every church were just like every other church. In diversity there can be real strength. For example, we have had many different kinds of Baptist congregations, some "Episcopalian" Baptist churches, and some "Holy Roller" Baptist churches, with the vast majority of them lying somewhere in between. To recognize this freedom of action and still to work in brotherly love will mean strength because all kinds of men will be served and God honored in a variety of ways. One plants, another waters, but God gives the growth. Our people live on wheels and there is no reason why they can't drive a few extra miles to serve God in a church that gives them the opportunity to do what they feel called to do for him and for their fellowmen. If a particular church provides the kind of worship which feeds their souls more than any other, that's where they should worship.

Worship Services Influenced by New Trends

For many years we have observed Youth Sunday and/or Youth Week. We have expected our young people to be little carbon copies of their elders in conducting worship. Do we dare turn them loose today? The worship committee would do well to consult with youth and work out with them a service that is really theirs. Let some of the older folks be shocked. They'll get over it, and will appreciate it more later. The simple use of contemporary language instead of Elizabethan anachronisms will sound harsh at first but will communicate more directly. The rock music will be particularly "out of place" but it has a way of getting down deep inside. And its loudness, enough to make one deaf, will give affirmation in no uncertain terms as well as a sense of immanence, importance, and power.

Youth Sunday was observed this year in a neighboring church and the young people worshiped God their way. It proved to be a great blessing to most of their parents and friends. Service No. 22 in the resource section is the order used. It is probably more structured than many youth would want, but it is the product of this particular group. (One page is shown.)

But the use of ideas and actions from the new style of worship has invaded the more formal and staid church services. On an Easter Sunday morning in a large First Baptist Church in a Southern city the worshipers were stimulated by the skillful use of trumpet and drum and the leadership of choirs in antiphonal reading as well as singing. They felt as never before the despair of the disciples who had just buried their Master and Friend. It came following a dramatic account in responsive readings of the crucifixion of Jesus, and a confession of their own sins and a pastoral prayer. It was then that a man stood up in the middle of the congregation and said in a loud voice: "Let's all go home now. It is finished. There is nothing more for us to do. His family is in tears. His friends have gone away. The man is dead. All's lost!" This service is reproduced as item No. 23.

The concern for congregational participation has influenced church architecture. Church leaders should realize that the kind of auditorium or sanctuary pretty well determines the life and worship of the church. An increasing number of groups of all denominations are building a church in the round in the effort to get everyone in on the action.

Worship committees and planning teams will need to use their best skills in picking and choosing those innovations of the more formal and more informal trends of our time.

5

Arranging and Printing Orders of Worship

The arrangement of the material in your worship folder will be determined by the needs of the people, the overall purpose of worship, and the immediate intent of that particular service. Your plan will have unity and continuity and will be designed to take the people as they are when they enter the house of the Lord and lead them step by step to where they should be. The outlines of the services included in this book for your benefit should give you good ideas on this important matter.

The different parts of worship stand out more prominently in some of the orders than in others. This is particularly true of Nos. 1, 10, 11, 13, 15, 20, and 23, although it is apparent in almost all of them on closer examination. Dr. Segler in his *Christian Worship* makes some excellent suggestions on outlines for worship and gives several examples of how it is done (pp. 190-193). The response of the creature to the Creator usually follows this pattern in order: Adoration, Confession, Thanksgiving, Exhortation, Dedication. They form an acrostic ACTED. And that is exactly what we are supposed to have done in worship. Too many of us are lackadaisical spectators.

The worship committee and planning team will spend all the time necessary in the selection and the arrangement of an outline of worship action to be used by their church for a certain period of time, from three months to a year. There will be special days of promotion and of devotion when the order will be abandoned temporarily, but the general outline will be usually followed for as long as the church desires. This means, then, that special care will be exercised in making so important a decision. Its inauguration should be preceded by careful preparation. Certainly the choir or choirs and the music leaders should have considerable to say about the outline selected. The reaction of several groups in the church family could be obtained before the final decision is made. It could be presented to the prayer meeting "fraternity," the officers and workers of the several organizations, the church council, and the diaconate. In this way the people will already have a large group familiar with and capable of leadership of worship using the order.

When the decision has been made on which outline to use the worship committee and/or planning team will prepare work sheets to be used by the various people who will contribute the items which will fill up the various parts. Item No. 24 is an example of such a work sheet. A considerable number will be duplicated. How many will depend on the duration of the time and number of people involved. They will be distributed to the pastor, minister of music, organist, minister of education, and perhaps others. They will first date them, and then add material to them in short- and long-range planning each according to his own responsibility. Then he will bring his file of work sheets to the planning meeting. These will constitute a wealth of suggestions needed by the planning team. Their work will not only be made much easier but it will be faster. And, most important, it will be of the highest quality of which the group is capable. Perhaps, the minister of music, for example, may have two or three selectons listed for each place where music is required. Then when he gets with the planning group and can see the direction in which the thought is moving he will know rather quickly which one of his alternatives will best fit the situation.

Each member of the planning team will keep a file of worship folders which have been used. He will pay particular attention to his own special responsibility, like the titles of sermons, names of anthems, hymns, and organ selections, to avoid duplication and to give the people a balanced diet. The simplest way to keep up with which hymns are being sung is to keep a hymnal just for that particular purpose. Each time a hymn is selected for use the date is put in the margin. When the hymn is suggested in the planning session a moment's examination will tell when it was sung last and how often it has been used.

If the pastor will share with other members of the team the sermon topics he expects to use in the next several weeks, the other members of the planning team can work on selections which will feature the same theme. In this way the arrangement will have harmony and strength.

Printing Orders of Worship

Every talent and trick of the printer's art should be used to make your worship fulfil the purpose for which it was intended: bring people into the presence of God as soon and as intently as possible. You should get some good ideas from the folders presented in this volume. They come from a variety of places and represent the skill of many people. You will be the judge consciously and unconsciously of each one of them. You will use only that which fits your purpose and situation.

If you can afford to have your bulletins printed by a firm that is used by successful business organizations you will be wise to do so. The Lord and the church are worthy of the best. People in business are convinced that it pays them to use the best stationery and advertising material available. Their clients are impressed by attractive messages and are repulsed by shoddy materials. A messy, hard to read worship folder depresses rather than inspires. We expect the house of the Lord to be clean and beautiful and worthy of him. The folder should be also. So the question ends up being: can we afford not to have the best?

Fortunately, duplicating and printing machines suitable for purchase by the churches have greatly improved in quality in the last few years. Many different types are available. There is one which your church can use that has been particularly designed for your tasks. Before the purchase is made by the group responsible for it the worship committee should be consulted. There is absolutely nothing that the church will use that machine for that is more important than the weekly production of one or more worship folders.

The persons responsible for printing the folder will put forth every effort to make it attractive. They should continually be on the lookout for new ideas for improvement. They will get them from the firm that sold them the machine, from the people who sell them supplies, from denominational bulletins and publications, and from special firms who make it their business to supply such information. The trading of folders between sister churches near and far is also quite a good idea. Geraldine Hess has written a very practical and helpful book on *Planning the Church Bulletin for Effective Worship.*

6

Conducting and Evaluating Worship Services

Much that we have already written has dealt directly or indirectly with these subejcts. But it should be of value to tie it together as we worship and evaluate in going through a service together. The order of worship is one that was used in a Baptist church on Pentecost Sunday, 1970. To plan a service just for this day is a good indication that those who are responsible for worship in this church are cognizant of the values of observing the Christian year and this particular day. The service is No. 25 in the resource section.

You will note that the people are encouraged to be in the sanctuary well before eleven o'clock so they may make individual preparation for worship and really be ready to go when the chiming of the hour is heard.

We catch ourselves using the word "sanctuary," which to some people is suspect. It was to our parents. It is right to be careful about the words we use. They stand for something and their use educates and informs us in a certain way of life. We should examine the word as to its derivation, its connotation, and as to what it means to others as well as ourselves. A sanctuary is a place sacred to God, a temple; it is a refuge to which one may flee for safety; it is a reservation where birds and animals are protected. "Sanctuary" is a biblical word. It is true that it has been and is now used by people who magnify ritual and sacraments and priests but this is no reason why we should turn the word over to them for their exclusive use as long as it's meaning is not inconsistent with our faith. Is "auditorium" better? It's more popular with some groups. But is it adequate? The house of the Lord is a place where we do more than listen.

It's interesting how some people cringe at the word "sanctuary" but glibly speak of the "chancel' choir. "Chancel" means, according to Webster, "the part of a church around the altar, usually at the east end, reserved for the use of the clergy and the choir: it is sometimes set off by a railing or lattice." The word itself originally meant lattices and crossbars. It is completely foreign to evangelical worship in derivation and meaning. Its message is that of division between the laity and the "religous."

The outline of service 25 is true to the purpose of the planners: Aspiration, Devotion, Instruction, Dedication, and Fellowship. It is not as faithful to the usual psychological pattern of worship as some outlines, but it certainly is not contrary to it. It is much closer to worship needs of us sinners at the beginning of the experience than the order of most Baptist churches. Unlike most Christians around the world Baptists generally don't give their people any encouragement or place to fulfil the deep need for confession and forgiveness until maybe the pastoral prayer, or perhaps the sermon.

The deep desire of the human heart for forgiveness is universal and ever present. Why do we neglect it? Primarily because our forefathers threw out the confession when they rejected the priestly absolution. The power of the Roman Catholic priest in this respect was as terrifying as it was unbiblical. But every Christian is a priest, and we need to confess our sins to one another and to God. And we certainly need to be forgiven. In the service under examination a young lady is leader and quotes the assuring words of Christ. The assurance of pardon may also be given by quoting any of many such verses in the Bible. One of the best known is 1 John 1:9.

The planning team may use another method for helping the people search their souls and get right with God. "The Preparation for Worship" may describe a life situation which speaks the language of the people and stabs them awake to their need for forgiveness—for God. Robert Raines's little book, *Creative Brooding,* has been expressly written for this very purpose.

Service No. 25 is begun with a hymn of praise. This is the chief function of a hymn as it is of worship—the praise of Almighty God. We are not amusing ourselves or primarily building up the fellowship. Our purpose is to glorify God. Hymns are also used as a medium of prayer, expressing adoration, invocation, confession and supplication, thanksgiving, and oblation. The last is illustrated in the hymn which is considered by some to be the most wonderful of all: "Were the whole realm of nature mine, That were a present far too small; Love so amazing, so divine, Demands my soul, my life, my all."

The psalms were the first hymns of the Christian church, and they have been sung for many centuries by most Christians. They are very seldom sung now by Baptists. The purpose of the Gloria Patri which is a part of the service now under examination is to turn a Jewish psalm into an act of Christian praise joining the old and new covenants. The churches of our time have a threefold heritage of hymnody: the Catholic tradition of St. Ambrose and the Middle Ages, reinforced by the Tractarians; it is heir also to the Puritan tradition at its best in Isaac Watts; and lastly to the evangelical tradition of the Moravians which flowered so beautifully in John and Charles Wesley.

The New English Bible is used in the reading of the Scriptures. Ordinarily a standard version of the Bible should be used in a service of this kind unless a translation has a striking phrase that will stimulate the people to see new light in God's truth. The translations are particularly useful for study. For example, we have chosen *Today's English Version* for this book *about* worship. The King James is incomparably valuable for worship, especially the more familiar Psalms.

It is interesting to observe the great differences there are in the amount of Scripture read and the quality of reading in the several churches and denominations. We have been in services where the Bible was not read at all. The pastor quoted his text and began its exposition. In most of the churches around the world selections are read from the Old Testament, from the Epistles, from the Gospels, and from the Psalms. A stated lectionary is followed in keeping with the Christian Year. This means that the people hear the great passages read every year and their souls are fed a balanced diet.

It is a strange contradiction that the very people who almost make the Bible an idol in their jealousy for its safety from all enemies are usually the ones that read it less in worship services and, in general, poorly. On the other hand, many who take a text and depart from it in giving some good advice for a sermon are the ones who read it more, and more intelligibly and beautifully. Why don't we choose the best of both worlds for ourselves? Skoglund, in his *Worship in the Free Churches,* gives an excellent discussion on the Christian Year, and follows it with a table of Scripture lessons for each Sunday (pp. 137-155). Segler's *The Broadman Minister's Manual* has valuable information on "The Christian Year and Church Calendar" (pp. 141-145).

Nine tenths of the Christians around the world pray the Lord's Prayer at every major service of worship. The majority of Southern Baptists will go a year or more without praying it. Our Lord gave it to us as a model. It has been a blessing to millions for hundreds of years. Why neglect it so? The answer is our traditional fear of ritualistic prayer—even if it belongs to Jesus and even though he gave it to us for our good. To pray it all the time, as some do, is probably to do it harm, but to neglect it entirely is to suffer great loss. We sing the same songs together over and over and feel they do us good. We would be blessed by praying together more.

There are three kinds of prayers, mainly, in this regard. There are the extemporaneous prayers, to which one has given no forethought. Our forefathers reacted against the second kind of prayer: the read prayer of ritual. They believed the Holy Spirit was in the former and not the latter. Isaac Watts, a free churchman, who was in the midst of this controversy, recommended the "conceived" prayer. By this he meant one that is thought and prayed through ahead of time and usually written out, but finally offered without manuscript.

In our opinion, the short prayers, like invocations, offertory prayers, and benedictions can best be given by memorizing the great prayers of Christian worship, or by reading them from small cards prepared for the purpose and kept on file. If one waits for the inspiration of the moment for these prayers he will likely find himself saying the same thing all the time.

But the pastoral prayer, we think, should be conceived in one's study as he meditates upon the goodness of God and the needs of his people. It should be seldom, if ever, read, and the mind and heart should be open to new thoughts and directions.

Although we know little about it we have always been inspired and helped by sacred music of great inspirational power which is offered just before the sermon. Pastor and people then have their minds on God and not on the preacher and his performance. The anthem sung by the choir is quite appropriate to the theme of the service. It is a good practice to print the words in the worship folder in understanding the message. An anthem that is full of gibberish and runs on too long can really hurt rather than help a service.

The congregation's attitude toward the pastor has already been greatly influenced by his life and his relation to them as friend and counselor. The way he began the service probably set the tone for all of it. His attitude was that of humility but he should be positive in speech. He doesn't say "May we pray," but "Let us pray."

The dress of the minister poses a real problem these days. If things continue to go as they are he may end up wearing a robe to escape a dilemma, and that would be a shock to many. The robe also magnifies his clerical role, which may influence congregational participation negatively. The problem is that we are in a state of rapid and radical change in men's clothes. If the minister dresses conservatively as clergymen have for years, he will set himself apart. If he goes in for the bright new colors, he will shock some and please the others, especially the youth. So the best road seems to be somewhere in between—in good taste—and so as not to distract from the main business of the hour.

As was stated above some Christians feel that every service of worship should be a service of the Lord's Supper or one that points to it. This is emphasized by putting the offering after the sermon. One should feel more in the spirit of dedication and sacrifice after hearing a good sermon. In this particular service the pastor goes from the prayer of dedication smoothly, without "Amen," while the people's heads are bowed, into the invitation to discipleship. A response to this invitation would mean an act of dedication and also of fellowship. After the new members are presented the benediction and choral response are followed by the chiming of twelve o'clock.

The hard work of the worship committee, the wise planning of the worship team, and the devoted service of many members of the congregation have, by God's grace, brought forth good fruit to his glory.

A SELECTED BIBLIOGRAPHY

Abba, Raymond. *Principles of Christian Worship*. New York and London: Oxford University Press, 1960.

Now in paperback, this is a popular book with seminary students. It has excellent chapters on the Ministry of the Word and Public Prayer.

Beasley-Murray, G. R. *Baptism in the New Testament*. London: Macmillan and Co., 1962.

For this outstanding work this Baptist scholar was signally honored by the Queen of England. It will open up whole new vistas in the understanding of Christian baptism for anyone who reads it with an open mind.

The Book of Common Prayer and Administration of the Sacraments and Other Rites and Ceremonies of the Church according to the Use of the Protestant Episcopal Church in the United States of America. New York: The Church Pension Fund, 1945.

Next to the Bible this book has influenced Christian worship for English-speaking peoples more than any other ever written.

Christensen, James L. *Contemporary Worship Services: A Sourcebook*. Old Tappan, N.J.: Fleming H. Revell Co., 1971.

An approach to the worship of God in the spirit, language and art forms of our time.

Clark, Neville. *Call to Worship*. London: SCM Press, 1960.

The story of how one British Baptist pastor led his people to more meaningful experiences of worship.

Davies, Horton. *Worship and Theology in England, from Watts and Wesley to Maurice, 1690–1850* Princeton, N.J.: Princeton University Press, 1961.

This volume, one of a series, is especially valuable for Free Churchmen since it covers the period of their beginnings in

England. It has a happy combination of thorough scholarship and attractive style for exciting reading.

Dobbins, Gaines S. *The Church at Worship*. Nashville: Broadman Press, 1962.

A very helpful and practical book. So far as we know it was the first of its scholarship and size published by Southern Baptists.

Eastwood, Cyril. *The Priesthood of All Believers*. London: The Epworth Press, 1960.

The subtitle is "An Examination of the Doctrine from the Reformation to the Present Day." Everybody talks about it and many brag about it. This book will show us how well we practice it.

Fosdick, H. E. *A Book of Public Prayers*. New York: Harper and Brothers, 1959.

Here is a very fine resource for the enriching of one's leading in public prayer. Excellent litanies are also given.

Hess, Geraldine. *Planning the Church Bulletin for Effective Worship*. New York: Exposition Press, 1962.

This is an excellent guide on how to prepare worship folders and make them creative in stimulating reverence and devotion.

Johnson, Alvin D. *Celebrating Your Church Anniversary*. Valley Forge: The Judson Press, 1968.

You don't need help like this too often but when you do you really need it. Here is an excellent book by one who writes from the experience of many such celebrations and doesn't miss a detail.

Lovelace, Austin C. and Rice, William C. *Music and Worship in the Church*. New York: Abingdon Press, 1968.

This is a complete text not only for the musicians but every member of the church.

Manson, T. W. *Ministry and Priesthood: Christ's and Ours.* London: The Epworth Press, 1958.

This little book (only two lectures) declares: "The ministry of Jesus is the standard and pattern of the Church's task; but, more than that, the Church's task is the continuation of the ministry of Jesus."

Moore, Edgar J. *A Guide to Music in Worship.* Great Neck, N.Y.: Channel Press, 1959.

This is a comprehensive, current and descriptive listing of sacred solos in print—classified by Bible verse and chapter used in text, and indexed for appropriateness to the church calendar.

Payne, E. A. and Winward, S. F. *Orders and Prayers for Church Worship.*

An excellent manual on worship prepared by two outstanding British Baptist leaders and scholars.

Raines, Robert A. *Creative Brooding.* New York: The Macmillan Company, 1966.

This book is not intended to comfort or even inspire, but rather to provoke thought and trigger action.

————. *The Secular Congregation.* New York: Harper and Row, 1968.

The author is concerned about the present division among Christians between those who look for God inside the church with its activities on the one hand, and on the other, the people who search for him outside the church in the world. He gives ideas about new forms of worship that will help draw these divergent groups together in a common purpose.

Segler, Franklin M. *Christian Worship: Its Theology and Practice*. Nashville: Broadman Press, 1967.

This is a scholarly and at the same time very practical and helpful book. It is valuable to anyone interested in worship. It should be required reading for every Southern Baptist who has the responsibility of planning and/or leading worship.

————. *The Broadman Minister's Manual*. Nashville: Broadman Press, 1968.

We predict that this manual will become standard for Southern Baptists and will remain so for at least a generation. It not only tells "how" but also "why" and is rich in resource material and sound advice.

Skoglund, John E. *A Manual of Worship*. Valley Forge, Pa.: The Judson Press, 1968.

An American Baptist scholar has prepared an excellent manual based on years of experience as a pastor leading worship and as a seminary professor teaching others how it should be done.

————. *Worship in the Free Churches*. Valley Forge, Pa.: The Judson Press, 1965.

The author is concerned about the trend on the part of some free church ministers and churches to forget their heritage in adopting non-evangelical worship practices. After pointing out the dangers of going in the wrong way he shows how worship may be enriched by insights from the practices of the Early Church and the Reformation.

Smith, B. F. *Christian Baptism: A Survey of Christian Teaching and Practice*. Nashville: Broadman Press, 1970.

The reading of this book should give the leader in worship at a baptismal service a wealth of knowledge and understanding to undergird his attitude and practice.

Underhill, Evelyn. *Worship*. New York: Harper and Brothers, 1937.

This classic of all books on the subject has gone through many editions and has been in paperback for years. It is a basic textbook on the nature, characteristics, principles, and practices of Christian worship of every sect and denomination.

Wallis, Charles L., ed. *The Table of the Lord: A Communion Encyclopedia*. New York: Harper and Brothers, 1958.

An excellent resource for a very special occasion.

————. *Worship Resources for the Christian Year*. New York: Harper and Brothers, 1954.

A well-selected treasury of helps of all kinds for planners of worship services.

Watkins, Keith. *Liturgies in a Time When Cities Burn*. Nashville: Abingdon Press, 1969.

As the title indicates this is an effort to fit the ritual, feeling, form, and practice of the times into a pattern of worship that is relevant for our disturbed age.

White, James F. *New Forms of Worship*. Nashville: Abingdon Press, 1971.

This is a book that endeavors to keep the best of the old forms and make the most of the new.

Winward, Stephen F. *The Reformation of Our Worship*. Richmond: John Knox Press, 1964.

This scholarly British Baptist pastor is vitally and fruitfully interested in worship as it should be practiced by a devout servant of God who makes the fullest use of the Christian tradition. He has a tendency toward the high church position.

RESOURCES

Resource 1

MORNING WORSHIP

This is our Father's House--the home of praise, prayer, and fellowship. May all who enter here find pardon, peace, and inspiration. May they give reverence, attention, and loving service.

PREPARATION FOR WORSHIP--

Repentance means a real and costly change of direction. Our present directions lead to the steep cliffs of destruction. A pointed story by Dr. Rufus Jones puts this rightabout-face clearly. A foot traveler asked a youth he saw by the wayside for the location of a destination he wished to reach. He received this answer, "If you go on the way you are headed it will be about 25,000 miles, but if you turn rightabout-face it will be about three."

--Halford E. Luccock

WE ENTER INTO WORSHIP - Eleven O'Clock
    Musical Meditation - "Sanctus"   Gounod
    *Congregational Hymn (32) - "Come, Thou Almighty King"   Giardini
    *Prayer of Invocation
    *Choir Response - "Lord, As We Thy Name Profess"
    Organ Interlude
WE HOLD CONVERSATION WITH GOD
    The Scripture Lesson - Mark 1:1-14
    Anthem - "Seek Ye the Lord"   Roberts
    The Morning Prayer
    Response by the Choir - "Let the Words of My Mouth"   Adiel
    *Response by the Congregation (150)
        "Spirit of God, Descend Upon My Heart"   Barnby
WE ENTER INTO PARTNERSHIP WITH GOD
    A Word of Welcome
    Offertory Sentence
    Organ Offertory - "On the Altar"   Smith
    Presentation of Tithes and Offerings
    *Prayer of Dedication
WE OPEN OUR MINDS TO GOD'S TRUTH
    Silent Prayer for God's Guidance of our Thought
    Sermon - "Time to Turn Around"   The Pastor
WE CONSECRATE OURSELVES TO GOD AND HIS WILL
    The Invitation to Membership
    *Hymn of Invitation (327) - "Take My Life and Let It Be" Bradbury
    *The Prayer of Benediction
    *Choral Benediction - "Threefold Amen"   Danish
WE GO FORTH WITH CHRIST TO LIVE AND TO SHARE THE ABUNDANT LIFE
    *Organ Postlude - "Recessional"   McDowell

*Congregation Standing

Celebration of Holy Communion

Eleven o'clock a.m.

As you enter the sanctuary, let talking cease and prayer begin.

The Organ:—"Jesus, Gentlest Saviour" . . . . . *Garth Edmundson*
Chiming of the Hour
Processional Hymn:—"Fairest Lord Jesus" . . . *Old Crusaders' Hymn*
Number 159

Call to Worship and Praise . . . . . . Mr. Johnson and Congregation
Have mercy upon me, O God, according to Thy lovingkindness; according unto the multitude of Thy tender mercies blot out my transgressions.
Wash me thoroughly from mine iniquity, and cleanse me from my sin.
Create in me a clean heart, O God, and renew a right spirit within me.
Cast me not away from Thy presence, and take not Thy Holy Spirit from me.
Restore unto me the joy of Thy salvation, and uphold me with Thy free spirit.
O Lord, open Thou my lips, and my mouth shall show forth Thy praise.

The Gloria Patri (Number 525) . . . . . . Congregation and Choir
The Invocation and Lord's Prayer . . . . Mr. Johnson and Congregation
Greetings and Invitation to Worship . . . . Minister

Reading of the Holy Scriptures . . . . Minister
The Pastoral Prayer and Choral Response . . . . Minister and Choir
Hymn of Remembrance:—"In memory of the Saviour's love" (Thomas Cotterill)
Number 393   *Alexander R. Reinagle*

The Service of Giving
The Offertory Sentence . . . . Minister
Offertory Anthem:—"Jesus, my Lord"   *George F. Handel, arranged by Walter Ehret*
The Senior Choir

Jesus, my Lord, my God, my All,
Hear me, blest Saviour, when I call;
From Thy dwelling place pour down, O Lord,
Pour down the riches of Thy grace.

Jesus, my Lord, I Thee adore;
O make me love Thee more and more.

Jesus, of Thee shall be my song;
To Thee my heart and soul belong;
All that I am or have is Thine,
And Thou, my Saviour, Thou art mine.

—Henry Collins

The Doxology . . . . Choir and Congregation
Offertory Dedication . . . . Minister

OBSERVANCE OF THE LORD'S SUPPER

Introductory Meditation . . . . Minister

Confession and Consecration . . . . . . Minister and Congregation
 God spake these words, and said: I am the Lord thy God; thou shalt have none other
  Gods but me.
 Help us, O God, to seek first Thy kingdom and Thy righteousness.
 Thou shalt not make to thyself any graven image, nor the likeness of anything that is in
  heaven above, or in the earth beneath, or in the water under the earth; thou shalt not
  bow down to them, nor worship them.
 **Whatever idols we have known, help us to tear them "from Thy throne, and worship only
  Thee."**
 Thou shalt not take the Name of the Lord thy God in vain.
 Help us to so live, O God, that our lives do not belie our profession.
 Remember that thou keep holy the Sabbath-day.
 Teach us that the Sabbath was made for man, and not man for the Sabbath.
 Honor thy father and thy mother.
 **May we especially honor them in the way we honor Thee and unselfishly serve our fellow-
  men.**
 Thou shalt do no murder.
 O Lord, help us rid our lives of hatred which can lead to this.
 Thou shalt not commit adultery.
 Guide us, O God, toward becoming pure in heart, mind, and body.
 Thou shalt not steal.
 **Lead us, our Father, in acknowledging the innate worth of every man created in Thine
  image, and in granting freedom of opportunity to all.**
 Thou shalt not bear false witness against thy neighbor.
 **Keep us, O God, from doing or saying anything that would be harmful to another. May
  we put away all bitterness, and wrath, and anger, and malice, and evil speaking.**
 Thou shalt not covet.
 **O Lord, teach us to be kind one to another, tenderhearted, forgiving one another, even
  as God for Christ's sake hath forgiven us. We beseech Thee to have mercy upon us,
  and write all these Thy laws in our hearts.**

Communion Hymn:—"When I survey the wondrous cross"

Breaking of Bread — Delivery
Prayer Hymn:—"Bread of Heaven" . . . . Choir
Partaking of Bread

Communion Meditation . . . . Minister

Pouring of Wine — Delivery
Prayer Hymn:—"Vine of Heaven" . . . . Choir
Partaking of Wine

Hymn of Commitment:—"Alas! and did my Saviour bleed?" (Isaac Watts)
      Number 101   *Hugh Wilson*
Benediction . . . . Minister
Response by the Congregation:—"The Lord's Prayer" . . *Albert Hay Malotte*
The Organ:—"Deck thyself, my soul, with gladness" . . . *Joseph W. Clokey*

All visitors are cordially invited to a Visitors' Reception in the church parlor at the
conclusion of this service.

The flowers in the sanctuary today are given to the glory of God and in loving memory of Mr. A.
Clyde Ferrell and Mr. A. Clyde Ferrell, Jr., by Mrs. Ferrell and Linda.

THE MINISTERS
R. F. Smith, Jr., Senior Minister

Leath C. Johnson, Education   *John T. Laverty, Music*
       Assistants
L. Alan Sasser, Pastoral   *H. Stephen Shoemaker, Youth*

Sympathy: We express Christian sympathy to the family of Mrs. W. A. Pope.

Resource 3

BAPTISM

O Lord, I come professing unto this water's side
That Thou art Christ my Saviour, my Master, and my Guide.
I now renounce all evil. To Thee I pledge my soul,
My life, and my devotion, as grace my faith enfolds.

This picture of Thy dying portrays my death to sin;
The likeness of Thy burial--myself immersed and cleansed.
Because Thou hast arisen, new life Thou gavest me.
I rise a new creation to live eternally.

The dove of peace descendeth, and love pervades my world.
The Lamb of God is watching, His hands with blood impearled.
The Spirit bids my shoulders to yoke with power Divine.
I now am Thy disciple; Thy life is my design.

                                        Helen Sims Smaw

Hymn tune: "O Jesus, I Have Promised" by Arthur H. Mann

A SERVICE OF BAPTISM

****

Organ Prelude

Welcome and Announcements

Call to Worship (Congregation)

"For as many as were baptized into Christ have put on Christ. There is neither Jew nor Greek, there is neither slave nor free, there is neither male nor female; for you are all one in Christ Jesus." (Gal. 3:27-28)

The Invocation

Hymn - "Wherever He Leads, I'll Go"

Responsive Reading

Evening Prayer

Hymn - "More Holiness Give Me"

Tithes and Offerings

Baptismal Meditation:
"We Are God's Children Now"

Solo: "O Jesus, I Have Promised"

Pledge of Candidates and Congregation

Hymn - "Something for Thee"

Baptism of Candidates

Hymn of Departure - "Blest Be the Tie"

Benediction

Organ Postlude

PLEDGE OF CANDIDATES AND CONGREGATION

(To Candidate:)

PASTOR: Do you come to be baptized because you want to identify your life with our Lord Jesus Christ?

CANDIDATE: I do.

PASTOR: Do you promise to be faithful to His way of life and to serve Him with all that you are and have?

CANDIDATE: I do.

(To Congregation:)

PASTOR: Do you as members of this congregation reaffirm your desire to follow the way of Christ?

CONGREGATION: We do.

PASTOR: Will you accept the ones who are to be baptized this evening as Christians and walk with them in the Christian way?

CONGREGATION: We will.

THE ORDINANCE OF BAPTISM

Organ Prelude
The Call to Worship
Hymn - "More Love to Thee, O Christ"

Announcements and Welcome
Hymn - "Trust and Obey"

The Offering

Scriptures: Jeremiah 31: 31-34
Romans 6: 3-14
Matthew 3: 11-17

Pastoral Meditation

The Vows:

Minister: Dearly Beloved, Baptism is an outward and visible sign of the grace of the Lord Jesus Christ, through which grace we become partakers of His righteousness and heirs of life eternal. Those receiving this Baptism are thereby marked as Christian disciples, and initiated into the fellowship of Christ's holy Church. Our Lord has expressly given to little children a place among the people of God, which holy privilege must not be denied them. Remember the words of the Lord Jesus Christ how he said, "Let the children come to me, do not hinder them; for to such belongs the Kingdom of God.":

Do you believe in God the Father, infinite in wisdom, goodness and love; and in Jesus Christ, his Son, our Lord and Saviour; and in the Holy Spirit, who taketh the things of Christ and revealeth them to us?

Candidates: We do.

Minister: Will you strive to know the will of God as taught in the Holy Scriptures, and to walk in the ways of the Lord, made known or to be made known to you?

Candidates: We will.

Minister: Do you confess your sins unto Almighty God, and putting your trust in Him, promise, in His strength, to follow His commandments and to walk from henceforth in His holy ways?

Candidates: We do

Minister: Do you seek to yield yourself unto God, that the same spirit which was in Jesus Christ may be in you, and that you may be his disciple not in name only but in deed and in truth?

Candidates: We do.

Minister: Let us pray.

THE CHURCH: (in unison) Almighty and everlasting God, receive and sanctify with thy Spirit these thy servants, now to be baptized into Jesus Christ according to thy word; may they find in thee their refuge, their strength, their wisdom and their joy. Keep them faithful to thee all the days of their lives that they may finally come unto thy everlasting kingdom; through Jesus Christ our Lord. Amen.

Hymn - "His Way with Thee"
Organ Interlude and Silent Prayer

THE ORDINANCE OF BAPTISM

The Benediction

The Postlude

A SERVICE OF BAPTISM

Organ Prelude

Hymn-_"I Am Thine, O Lord"
Announcements and Welcome

Choral Worship - "Bless the Lord, O My Soul"

Responsive Reading - "Meaning of Baptism" - Broadman Hymn #38
Evening Prayer
Hymn - "Living for Jesus"

Tithes and Offerings

Baptismal Meditation - THE REMINDERS OF BAPTISM

Pledge of Candidates and Congregation

Hymn - "I Gave My Life for Thee"
Baptismal Prayer

Baptism of Candidates

Hymn of Departure - "Blest Be the Tie"
Benediction

     ***   ***   ***   ***   ***

PLEDGE OF CANDIDATES AND CONGREGATION

(To Candidates:)

PASTOR: Do you come to be baptized to show your love to Christ and to follow His command?

CANDIDATE: I do.

PASTOR: Do you promise to be faithful to God and to His church?

CANDIDATE: I do.

(To Congregation:)

PASTOR: Do you accept the testimony of the ones who are to be baptized tonight?

CONGREGATION: We do.

PASTOR: Do you rededicate your lives to the principles and vows taken at your baptism?

CONGREGATION: We do.

PASTOR: Do you promise to accept the responsibility of giving direction to the new members of our fellowship as they grow in their Christian experience?

CONGREGATION: We do.

Resource 7

SERVICE OF THE LORD'S SUPPER

"Our heavenly Father, we thy humble children invoke thy blessing for this hour of worship. We adore thee, whose name is
love, whose nature is compassion, whose presence is joy, whose
spirit is goodness, whose holiness is beauty, whose will is
peace, whose service is perfect freedom, and in the knowledge
of whom standeth our eternal life. Unto thee be all honor and
all glory, through Jesus Christ our Lord. Amen."

+   +   +   +

Organ Prelude: "Reverie Religieuse" . . . . Clark
Call to Worship . . . . Choir and Minister
+The Gloria Patri . . . . Choir and Congregation

+HYMN OF PRAISE: NO. 313 . . . . Wyeth
                   "Come Thou Fount"
Organ Interlude
Reading of the Holy Scriptures: Matthew 5:3-16 . . . Minister
The Morning Prayer . . . . Minister

THE SERVICE OF GIVING
    The Offertory Sentence
    The Offertory Prayer
    The Offertory
    +The Doxology

THE SERMON - "We Break Bread Together" . . . . Minister

+HYMN OF FELLOWSHIP: NO. 354 . . . . Vail
                   "Close to Thee"
INVITATION TO THE LORD'S TABLE

THE WORDS OF INSTITUTION

SILENT PRAYER OF CONFESSION

PRAYER FOR PARDON AND BLESSING

THE DISTRIBUTION OF THE BREAD

THE HYMN OF TRUST
    (To be sung after the deacons return to the table)
    My faith looks up to Thee, Thou Lamb of Calvary, Saviour Divine.
      Now Hear me while I pray, Take all my guilt away,
    O let me from this day Be wholly Thine. Amen.

THE DISTRIBTUION OF THE WINE
   (Cups will be held in hand until Prayer of Dedication is
      concluded.)

THE HYMN OF DEDICATION
   (To be sung after the deacons return to the table)
   Just as I am without one plea
   But that Thy blood was shed for me;
   O Lamb of God, I come, I come. Amen.

THE PRAYER OF DEDICATION

HYMN OF FELLOWSHIP: NO. 366
                        "Blest Be the Tie"

SILENT PRAYER

PRAYER OF BENEDICTION

Organ Postlude

+The congregation is requested to stand.

NEW ROAD BAPTIST CHURCH, OXFORD.
Order of Service for Holy Communion.

Call to Worship
Hymn
Prayer of Confession
The Lord's Prayer
Notices
The Old Testament Lesson
Psalm
The New Testament Lesson
Sermon
Hymn
Prayers of Intercession

The Offertory
Offertory Prayer

Hymn

Words of Institution
Prayer of Thanksgiving
Communion

Hymn
Blessing

In this first part of the service we draw near to God in praise, repentance and trust. The children will leave at the end of it for their own classes.

In this second part of the service we hear God speaking to us through His Word and in the Sermon. Our response is two-fold: in praise for God's revelation of Himself, and in prayer both for ourselves and for others. The Notices remind us of things which concern us as the family of God, and may give added relevance to the prayers that follow.

In this third part of the service action is more important than words. We first offer our gifts to God; they are the symbols of ourselves, our lives and our labours, however unworthy. When the stewards bring our offerings to the Table we stand, thus identifying ourselves with our gifts, and remain standing while these gifts, along with the Bread and Wine, are offered to God.

All who love the Lord Jesus Christ are invited to take Communion. Any who do not wish to do so are welcome to stay without partaking; if, however, they prefer to leave, they should do so during this hymn. The action of the Communion continues as we follow the example of our Lord who, when he had taken the bread, gave thanks, break it and gave it to his disciples. In the great prayer of thanksgiving we bless God for our redemption through Christ, and pray that He will come among us now to transform our lives through His. We partake of the bread individually as we receive it; we retain the Cup until all are served and drink together. Thus we signify both the individual and corporate nature of our Communion.

MORNING WORSHIP : ELEVEN O'CLOCK
SUNDAY, AUGUST 28, 1966

\+   \+   \+

Prelude: "My Inmost Heart Now Yearneth" Buxtehude

Chiming of the Hour . . . . .Organist

PROCESSIONAL HYMN NO. 40 . . . . Luther
        "A MIGHTY FORTRESS IS OUR GOD"

CALL TO WORSHIP AND PRAISE

MINISTER: Christ our passover is sacrificed
    for us: therefore let us keep the feast,
PEOPLE: Not with the old leaven, nor with
    the leaven of malice and wickedness; but with
    the unleavened bread of sincerity and truth.

The Gloria Patri . . . . . Choir and Congregation
Invocation-Lord's Prayer . .Minister-Congregation

Greetings and Invitation to Worship . . .Minister

Anthem: "Peace I Leave With You" . . . . .Maxwell

    Peace I leave with you,
    My peace I give unto you.
    Not as the world giveth, give I unto you.

    Let not your heart be troubled,
    Neither let it be afraid.
    If you love me, keep my commandments.

    I will not leave you comfortless,
    I will come to you.

Reading of the Holy Scriptures . . . . .Minister
Prayer Meditation . . . . Organist
Pastoral Prayer . . . . Minister
Choral Response . . . . .Chancel Choir

HYMN NO. 129 . . . . .Glaser
            "O FOR A THOUSAND TONGUES"

WORSHIPPING WITH TITHES AND OFFERINGS
    Offertory Sentence . . . . .Minister
    Offertory Solo . . .Miss Betty Jane Foster
        "His Eye Is On the Sparrow"
    Offertory Dedication and Choral Response

CELEBRATION OF THE LORD'S LAST SUPPER
    Introductory Meditation . . . . . .Minister
    Prayer of Confession and Consecration
    Communion Hymn . . . . . . "Though Your Sins"

    Breaking of Bread - - Delivery
    Prayer Hymn: "Break Thou the Bread" . . Choir
    Partaking of Bread

    Communion Meditation . . . . Minister

    Pouring of Wine -- Delivery
    Prayer Hymn: "O Sacred Head" . . . . .Choir
    Partaking of Wine

    Concluding Meditation . . . . . . .Minister
    Prayer of Thanksgiving

HYMN OF INVITATION: NO. 366 . . . . . . Nageli
            "BLEST BE THE TIE"

Doxology . . . . .Choir and Congregation
Chiming of the Hour . . . . Organist
Postlude: "Now Thank We All Our God" . .Kaufmann
    +   +   +
The Minister will greet the Congregation at the
back of the Sanctuary.

MORNING WORSHIP - ELEVEN O'CLOCK
October 2, 1966

WORSHIP THROUGH PREPARATION
    The Prelude
    The Invitation to Worship
 * The Hymn of Praise 465: "God of Grace and God of
      Glory"   Hughes
    The Invocation, The Lord's Prayer, Gloria Patri
WORSHIP THROUGH MEDITATION AND EXALTATION
 * The Organ Meditation
    The Reading of the Scripture   Ephesians 2:11-22
    Ministry of Silent Confession - Pastoral Prayer -
    Choral Response
WORSHIP THROUGH GIVING
 * Hymn 48: "There's a Wideness in God's Mercy"
                                               Tourjee
    The Offertory Sentence and Offering
    The Anthem: "O Holy Jesu"   Lvoff
    The Doxology
WORSHIP THROUGH PROCLAMATION
    The Prayer
    The Sermon: The Communion of Saints   Minister
WORSHIP THROUGH DEDICATION
    Invitation to Christian Discipleship
    Hymn 443: "In Christ There Is No East or West"
                                              Reinagle
WORSHIP THROUGH COMMUNION
    The Words of Preparation   I Corinthians 11:27-32
    The Invitation
    The Scripture   I Corinthians 11:23-24
    The Prayer
    The Distribution of the Bread
    Silent Meditation: "Sustain me, O God, for I cast
      not only my burden but myself upon Thee."
    The Scripture   I Corinthians 11:25-26
    The Prayer
    The Distribution of the Cup
    Silent Meditation:"Thou hast borne my sorrows and
      sins;in Thy strength I shall live a new life."
    Hymn 366: "Blest Be the Tie"   Nageli-Mason
    The Postlude

82

Resource 11

MORNING WORSHIP SERVICE
November 8, 1970
This Service will proceed without announcement.

THE SERVICE OF PRAISE

Prelude — "Meditation, Op. 14" .... *Bubeck*

Introit — "O Come, Let Us Sing Unto the Lord" .... *Smith*

***Hymn of Praise — No. 574: "Turn Back, O Man" ....*(Old 124th)*
The Corporate Prayer
> O God of Christ:
> Touch us with Thy Presence.
> Renew us with Thy Word.
> Encourage us with Thy Grace.
> And embrace us with Thy Mission.
> Amen.

The Prayer of Private Confession and Choral Amen

The Service of Baptism

Minister to Candidate:	Are you here to be baptized into Christ and His Church, thus confessing Him as your Savior and Lord?"
Candidate	I am.
Minister:	Fellow members in Christ, you will acknowledge this baptism as your act of faith, thus promising to be a community of nurture and love?
Congregation:	We will.
Minister:	I baptize you in the name of the Father and the Son and the Holy Spirit.

***Hymn of Faith — No. 428: "Strong Son of God, Immortal Love"
(St. Crispin)

Prayer of Thanksgiving, Petition, and Intercession
***

THE SERVICE OF THE WORD

Anthem: "Upon this Rock" .... *John Ness Beck*
(**The Congregation is requested to stand and join in singing.)

Upon this rock I will build my church;
And the gates of hell shall not prevail against it.
I will give thee the keys of the Kingdom of Heaven.
And whatsoever thou shalt bind on earth shall be bound in Heaven.
And whatsoever thou shalt loose on earth shall be loosed in Heaven.

Lo, the winter is past; the rain is over and gone;
The flowers appear on the earth; the time of the singing of birds has come.
Arise and come away!

**The church's one foundation is Jesus Christ her Lord;
She is His new creation by water and the word;
From Heav'n He came and sought her to be His holy bride;
With His own blood He bought her, and for her life He died.

**Yet she on earth hath union with Father, Spirit, Son,
And mystic sweet communion with those whose rest is won;
O happy ones and holy! Lord, give us grace that we,
Like them the meek and lowly, on high may dwell with Thee.

                                                                    Amen.

The Reading of the Scripture............................*Matthew 6:5-6*

The Sermon — "And When You Pray"........................Mr. Carr

THE SERVICE OF DEDICATION

Hymn of Commitment — No. 342: "O Jesus, Thou Art Standing"
                                                            (*St. Hilda*)

The Offertory — "Cantabile"....................................*Clokey*

The Lord's Supper

The Doxology

The Congregational Covenant

> And now O God we promise and covenant, before Thee and in the presence of one another, to share the joy of Thy salvation with a broken world. Amen

The Benediction

The Gloria Patri

Organ Postlude

***Ushers will seat those waiting.

Members of the brass and percussion ensemble accompanying the choir this morning are students in the Wake Forest University Department of Instrumental Music.

The Service of Baptism will be observed this morning during the morning worship hour. Those to be baptized are as follows: Amy Barnett, Anne Bird, Jane Bird, Jimmy Cain, Carolyn Christman, Roy Garrison, Chip Hamrick, Heidi Hatfield, David Pulley, Ellen Robinson, Betty Seelbinder, Judy Tyndall, Beth Williard, Grant Williard, and Lou Ann Woods.

We would like to extend a cordial welcome to MRS. T. SLOANE GUY, SR. and the REV. and MRS. T. SLOANE GUY, JR. who joined our church last Sunday. They come to us by letter from the First Baptist Church of New Orleans, Louisiana.

There will be a meeting of the RETREAT PLANNING COMMITTEE this afternoon at 4:00 in Room 110. All 6 members are urged to attend.

This Service is broadcast over WFDD-FM, 88.5 MC. (Dormitory students who do not have FM radios can hear WFDD at 650 on their AM radios.)

Resource 12

A SERVICE OF WORSHIP FOR

A S H   W E D N E S D A Y

Preparation for Worship

1. Significance of "Ash Wednesday" - This day is observed by the vast majority of Christians of the West as a day of self-examination and repentance. It begins the period of Lent, a period of forty days (and intervening Sundays) given to fasting and prayer and meditation upon the sufferings of Jesus and his crucifixion for our salvation.

2. Special concerns for today - The confession of our sins, followed by repentance and an effort at restitution; prayers connected with the war in Viet Nam, social injustice at home, and the state of the Church.

3. Suggested readings in The Baptist Hymnal - Selections 65, 75

Organ Prelude-   "Ah, Holy Jesus"------------------------- Gruger
                              Professor Max Smith

Call to Worship

The Collect (Minister and People)
  Almighty and everlasting God, who hatest nothing that thou hast made, and dost forgive the sins of all those who are penitent; Create and make in us new and contrite hearts, that we, worthily lamenting our sins and acknowledging our wretchedness, may obtain of thee, the God of all mercy, perfect remission and forgiveness; through Jesus Christ our Lord, Amen.

Responsive Reading - "A Sinner's Confession"-------------No. 11

Solo -   "He Was Despised" ---------------Handel
                              Mrs. Eugene Owens

A General Confession (Minister and People)
  Almighty and most merciful Father; we have erred, and strayed from thy ways like lost sheep. We have followed too much the devices and desires of our own hearts. We have offended against thy holy laws. We have left undone those things which we ought to have done; And we have done those things we ought not to have done; And there is no health in us. But thou, O Lord, have mercy upon us, miserable offenders. Spare thou those, O God, who confess their faults. Restore thou those who are penitent; According to thy promises declared unto mankind in Christ Jesus our Lord. And grant, O most merciful Father, for his sake; that we hereafter live a godly, righteous, and sober life, To the glory of thy holy Name. Amen.

Assurance of Forgiveness (Minister and People)
  If we confess our sins, he is faithful and just to forgive us our sins, and to cleanse us from all unrighteousness.

Congregational Hymn - "I Lay My Sins on Jesus"----------No. 210

Responsive Reading - "The Nation" ---------------------No. 66

Prayers of Intercession

Congregational Hymn - "O God, We Pray for All Mankind"---No. 456

Prayer of Benediction

Organ Postlude - "All Glory Laud and Honor" -------------Teschner

A SERVICE OF WORSHIP
The Words From The Cross

12 Noon   **Good Friday**   **April 12, 1968**

SACRED ORGAN MUSIC   RICHARD FOSTER, *Organist*
THE CALL TO WORSHIP   THE REV. EDWARD B. WILLINGHAM, D.D.

> Minister: Is it nothing to you, all ye that pass by?
> People: Behold and see if there be any sorrow like unto his sorrow.
> Minister: God commendeth His love toward us in that, while we were yet sinners, Christ died for us.
> People: Behold the Lamb of God which taketh away the sin of the world.

THE INVOCATION (Here let the people unite with the Minister in prayer)
> Assist us mercifully with Thy help, O Lord of our salvation, that we may enter with joy upon the meditation of those mighty acts, whereby Thou hast given unto us life and immortality; through Jesus Christ our Lord. Amen.

FORGIVENESS AT THE CROSS

The First Word—"Father, Forgive Them For They Know Not What They Do"   St. Luke 23:32-38

A HYMN NUMBER 281: Jesus Calls Us   Galilee
THE MEDITATION
THE PRAYER (All Uniting)
> Almighty and everlasting God, who art always more ready to hear than we to pray, and art wont to give more than either we desire or deserve; pour down upon us the abundance of Thy mercy; forgiving us those things whereof our conscience is afraid and giving us those good things which we are not worthy to ask, but through the merits and meditation of Jesus Christ, Thy Son, our Lord. Amen.

AUTHORITY AT THE CROSS

The Second Word—"Today Shalt Thou Be with me in Paradise." St. Luke 23:39-43

A HYMN NUMBER 308: O Jesus I Have Promised   Angel's Story
THE MEDITATION
SPECIAL MUSIC   David Griffith
THE PRAYER (All Uniting)
> O Thou who art Love, and who seest all the suffering, injustice, and misery which reign in this world; have pity, we implore Thee, on the work of Thy hands. Look mercifully upon the poor, the oppressed and all who are heavy laden with error, labor, and sorrow. Fill our hearts with deep compassion for those who suffer, and hasten the coming of Thy Kingdom of justice and truth; through Jesus Christ our Lord. Amen.

REMEMBRANCE AT THE CROSS

The Third Word—"Woman! Behold Thy Son" "Son, Behold Thy Mother." St. John 19:25-27

A HYMN NUMBER 331: What a Friend   Erie

THE MEDITATION

THE PRAYER (All Uniting)

Infinite and eternal Spirit, our God and our Father, Author of all good, and never far from any of Thy children, we draw near to Thee, that in fellowship with Thee we may receive of Thy Spirit. May all the bonds of love and ties of friendship be made stronger and sweeter through Him who in His mortal agony was not unmindful that we need one another's love; even Jesus Christ our Lord. Amen.

SUBMISSION AT THE CROSS

The Fourth Word—"My God, My God, Why Hast Thou Forsaken Me?" St. Mark 15:33-34

A HYMN NUMBER 333: In The Hour Of Trial   Penitence

THE MEDITATION

SPECIAL MUSIC   David Griffith

THE PRAYER (All Uniting)

O almighty God, who art a strong Tower to all those who put their trust in Thee, to whom all things in heaven, in earth, and under the earth, do bow and obey, be now and evermore our Defense, and make us know and feel that there is none other Name under the heavens given to man, in whom and through whom we may receive health and salvation, but only the Name of Thy Son, our Lord Jesus Christ. Amen.

SUFFERING AT THE CROSS

The Fifth Word—"I Thirst." St. John 19:28-29

A HYMN NUMBER 235: Beneath The Cross   St. Christopher

THE MEDITATION

THE PRAYER (All Uniting)

Almighty God, whose most dear Son went not up to joy, but first He suffered pain, and entered not into glory before He was crucified; mercifully grant that we, walking in the way of the Cross, may find it none other than the way of life and peace; through Jesus Christ our Lord. Amen.

87

VICTORY AT THE CROSS

The Sixth Word—"It is finished". St. John 19:30

A HYMN NUMBER 228: When I Survey   Hamburg

THE MEDITATION

SPECIAL MUSIC   David Griffith

THE PRAYER (All Uniting)

Thou Forgiver of Sin, Healer of Sorrow, Vanquisher of Death, draw us unto Thyself, who art our Salvation and our all-conquering Hope. Make us citizens of Thy Kingdom, men of invincible goodwill, builders of a world where righteousness shall reign, and the law of love shall triumph over hate and strife. Hasten the day when Thou shalt take unto Thyself Thy great power and reign. Increase in us true devotion unto Thyself, nourish us with all goodness, and of Thy great mercy keep us steadfast; through Jesus Christ our Lord. Amen.

CONFIDENCE AT THE CROSS

The Seventh Word—"Father, Into Thy Hands I Commend My Spirit"   St. Luke 23:44-49

A HYMN NUMBER 237: In The Cross of Christ   Rathbun

THE MEDITATION

THE PRAYER (All Uniting)

Almighty God, who alone gave us the breath of life, and alone canst keep alive in us the holy desires Thou dost impart; we beseech Thee, for Thy compassion's sake, to sanctify all our thought and endeavors; that we may neither begin an action without a pure intention nor continue it without Thy blessing. And grant that, having the eyes of the mind opened to behold things invisible and unseen, we may in heart be inspired by Thy wisdom, and in work be upheld by Thy strength, and in the end be accepted of Thee as Thy faithful servants; through Jesus Christ our Saviour. Amen.

THE BENEDICTION

THE POSTLUDE

Resource 14

The Challenge of the Cross

Six o'clock p.m.

Organ Prelude
Processional Hymn: — "In the cross of Christ I glory" (John Bowring)
Number 100   Ithamar Conkey
Anthem: — "All in the April evening" (Katherine Tynan) Hugh S. Roberton

Presentation of the Special Feature, "THE CHALLENGE OF THE CROSS"
Revised by Paul Dell   by Charles A. Marsh

Directed by Mrs. Claude B. Williams, Jr.

Cast of Characters

Messenger . . . . Mrs. Alonzo A. Gregory
First disciple . . . . Mrs. John T. Laverty
Second disciple . . . . Bill Howard
Third disciple . . . . Mrs. Leath C. Johnson
Fourth disciple . . . . J. T. Craig, Jr.
Fifth disciple . . . . Mrs. Richard Dickinson
Sixth disciple . . . . Lloyd Pendergraft

Hymn of Challenge: — "Take up thy cross" (C. W. Everest) . *Roger C. Wilson*
Sung by Linda Swain, Soprano

The Service of Giving
Prayer of Dedication . . . . **Minister**
Receiving of Tithes and Offerings
Hymn of Dedication: — "Wherever He leads I'll go" . *B. B. McKinney*
Number 347, sung by the Choir

Benediction and Choral Response . . . . . . **Minister and Choir**
Organ Postlude

SUNDAY EVENING, 6:45 P.M. — Church Training Program

Everything You Always Wanted to Know about Witnessing, Room 154

Senior High Drama Group, Morgan Fellowship Hall

✤ ✤ ✤

"MY CHURCH NIGHT"

Wednesday Evening, April 14, 5:00 to 8:15 o'clock

A correlated program of church activities for the entire family

Supper in the Church Cafeteria (Morgan Hall), 5:00 to 6:30

The Prayer and Praise Service in Morgan Hall at 6:45

Finance Committee and Youth Council Meetings at 7:30

THE EVENING WORSHIP

6:30 p.m.-Training Union
7:30 p.m.- The Church at Worship

PRELUDE
THE SERVICE OF PRAISE
  Call To Worship
  Invocation
  *Hymn No. 461-"Jesus, Thy Boundless Love to Me"--------Gerhardt-Hemy
  Evening Prayer
THE SERVICE OF MEDITATION AND GIVING
  *Hymn No. 443-"O Jesus, I Have Promised"--------------------Bode-Mann
  Prayer of Dedication
  Evening Offering
THE SERVICE OF DEACON ORDINATION
  Scripture
  Sermon
  Installation
  Prayer of ordination
  The Laying on of Hands
THE DEACONS' PLEDGE
*Hymn No. 490-"Blest Be the Tie That Binds"-----------Fawcett-Mason
THE HAND OF FELLOWSHIP
*PRAYER OF BENEDICTION
ORGAN POSTLUDE

THE DEACON'S PLEDGE

The unbroken succession of the hands of ordination reaches back
across the centuries to the time of the Apostles signifying a covenant
in Christ to which I affirm my sincere loyalty.

As an ordained deacon of the Zebulon Baptist Church I dedicate myself to the fulfillment of the trust placed in me by my fellow members
whom I will serve, andI pledge that to the best of my ability:

I will live an exemplary Christian life according to the teachings
of the New Testament so that those who follow my example will not be
led into error.

I will hold in highest esteem the reputation of my church, subscribe
to and promote its doctrines, defend its liberty, encourage the extension of its world-wide mission, work for the salvation of the lost,
and support its pastor and those who are itsselected leaders.

I will accept such responsibilities in the church program as are
in keeping with my talents and ever seek to increase my capacity to
serve my Lord and His People.

I will hold inviolate all information given to me in confidence by
my pastor and other deacons and will consider all discussion and
comment pertaining to the church and its affairs as a sacred trust.

I will attend with faithfulness the services and worship and prayer,
the meetings of the deacons, the teaching and training programs in my
church, and absent myself from those functions only when in clear,
Christian conscience I may do so.

I will strive to understand more fully, through Bible study and
prayer, the Scriptural teaching that deacons are to be "men of good
report."

I will engage neither in the sale nor use of intoxicating drinks
as a beverage.

I will contribute to the support of my church keeping in mind the
teaching of the Scripture as to the portion of my substance that is
an acceptable gift.

I will ever strive for the advancement of the Kingdom of God and I
will not assume that the termination of my tenure of active service
as a deacon releases me from this pledge.

A SERVICE OF ORDINATION
on behalf of
James Edwin McSwain

Double Springs Baptist Church   January 24, 1971
Route 4, Shelby, North Carolina   3:00 P.M.

THE ORDER OF WORSHIP

Organ Prelude

Spoken Call to Worship –
O Come, let us worship and bow down: let us kneel
before the Lord our Maker. For He is our God; and
we are the people of His pasture, and the sheep of
His hand.

*Hymn of Praise "God, Our Father We Adore Thee"   No. 5

Invocation and Introductory Statement   C. A. Kirby, Jr.

The Reading of the Scripture   James P. Wall

The Sermon of Ordination   Dr. John T. Wayland

The Charge to the Candidate   Jack A. Bracey

The Prayer of Ordination   J. Colin Harris

Message in Music   D. Jack Heath
"Lord, Make Us Instruments"

Unison Reading "How Can I Be An Instrument For God?"

The Laying on of Hands

The Presentation of the Bible   C. A. Kirby, Jr.

*Hymn of Commitment "God of Grace and God of Glory" No.465

The Prayer of Benediction   James E. McSwain

Organ Postlude

(*Congregation will please stand)

Unison Reading

"HOW CAN I BE AN INSTRUMENT FOR GOD?"
by J. Harley Cecil

Leader: Lord, make me an instrument of your peace.

PEOPLE: How can I be an instrument of peace in such a mad, messed-up world?

Leader: By giving yourself to others. By seeking to console, to understand, to love, to give, to forgive, and to try to live the Good life.

PEOPLE: How do I begin?

Leader: By sharing feelings helpfully with other individuals in the everyday give-and-take realities of life.

PEOPLE: Then I should earnestly seek to bring some consolation to someone else more than I seek my own comfort.

Leader: Yes. You respond to every chance to communicate some meaningful message to others in their hurts, joys, failures, and successes.

PEOPLE: My message may need to be said in words; or it may need to be felt and left unsaid.

LEADER AND PEOPLE:
WE NEED THE GRACE TO KNOW WHEN TO SPEAK AND WHEN TO REMAIN SILENT IF WE OFFER THIS MINISTRY.

Leader: As a representative of God, you will want to try to understand others.

PEOPLE: And instead of yelling, "Nobody understands me", I will spend my energies gaining insight into someone else's circumstances.

LEADER AND PEOPLE:
DEVELOPING SUCH SENSITIVITY TO OTHER PERSONS WILL RESULT INTO EXPRESSIONS OF LOVE.

PEOPLE: Like with my genuine feelings of compassion, tenderness, and personal warmth.

Leader: And with special efforts to lift the quality of the atmosphere around you.

PEOPLE: Even my presence creates refreshment, positive attitudes and enthusiasm. My countenance offers encouragement to those who need to hear me say: "You are important. You have a special contribution to make to life."

Leader: Sincere "drawing out" like this will help awaken courage within those persons who need to discover their unique value in God's design for life.

LEADER AND PEOPLE: THIS IS LOVE.

Leader: As you give love in this way, you will receive fulfillment of your own needs.

PEOPLE: You mean the gift of myself will be accepted. I will become useful.

Leader: Yes, and this is never more true than when you share in the special needs of ordinary folks.

PEOPLE: What do you mean?

Leader: They need the help you can give. You need their return gifts of wisdom, genuineness, simple beauty, and the solid values they can teach you.

LEADER AND PEOPLE: THEN MY GOAL IS TO BECOME SO INVOLVED IN SHARING THAT I FORGET WHO IS THE GIVER AND WHO IS THE RECEIVER.

Leader: As we search for ways to be instruments of peace, we maintain human relationships in which harmony is a Christian characteristic.

PEOPLE: And I don't lie awake at night reviewing my grudges and counting the ways to "get even."

Leader: Rather, we surprise our avenger by giving him what he needs - our forgetfulness of the past, and our desire to begin all over again.

LEADER AND PEOPLE: OUR KINDNESS WILL BE SO OVERWHELMING THAT DIFFERENCES WILL BE FORGOTTEN.

PEOPLE: But it's not easy for some parts of my human-ness to give way so that I can be born to the Good Life.

Leader: No. There must be some special effort on your part if your hate is to die and make room for your caring as a Christian.

PEOPLE: My "don't care" attitude will give way to a Christ-like concern that has a certain vitality to it.

Leader: And your enduring faith and hope will grow to be stronger than your waning doubt and despair, although you may always have to live with some degree of these.

PEOPLE: I am beginning to see that as a potential instrument for God that I have many facets for development and continuous growth.

Leader: Like - peace, love, forgiveness, faith, hope, light, and joy.

LEADER AND PEOPLE: AND THESE VIRTUES OF LIFE ARE ALL TO BE MAINTAINED AS VITAL WORKING PARTS WITHIN ME IF I AM TO BE AN INSTRUMENT FOR GOD.

Resource 17

PRAYER INSTRUCTIONS
(Please follow these suggestions step by step.)

1. Read the passage marked in Red in the open Bible, II Chronicles 7:14. Read it again slowly.

2. Think about your wicked ways - We all have some though perhaps many are not conscious of them. Ask God to help you see everything in your life that is displeasing to Him. Take your time. Think it through. Give God a chance to speak to you. Have the people in our homes or at work seen anything in us that dishonors God?

3. Now after this period of self-examination ask yourself "Am I willing to turn away from my wicked ways?"
Please don't go to the next step until you have taken time to think this through. This is one of the important conditions which God's people must meet before He can give us a revival. Your happiness, peace and well-being as a Christian depends upon your attitude ot true repentance.

4. Now read the passage marked in red from the small Bible, I John 1:9. You see, if you sincerely repent and confess your sins, God says that He will forgive you and cleanse you.

5. Do you really want a revival?
Read II Chronicles 7:14 again - note what we are to do and what God says that He will do.

6. Pray for a revival.

7. Turn in the Baptist Hymnal to Responsive Reading No. 46.
Read the selection slowly. Don't be in a hurry. If you need an hour, take it. The next person will not mind your staying over.

8. Pray for the pastor.

9. Pray for the Evangelist.

10. Now look at the copy of the Ashley Heights Baptist Church Sunday School Census. Read the summary on the first page. Look at the names on the next pages. Do you know some of these people who are lost?

11. Now read Responsive Reading No. 42 from the Hymnal.

12. Pray for the lost.
Why not make a prayer list? There are some plain cards and a pencil on the back of the first pew - use them.

13. Will you promise God that you will try to win at least one person to faith in the Saviour during these next two weeks?

14. Ask God to help you win that lost person.

15. Please do not leave until the next person comes.

16. Suggest to the next person that you have a brief prayer together before you go.

H. L. Summerford

ORDER OF WORSHIP
DEDICATION OF NEW SANCTUARY
May 4, 1969   Two O'Clock

ORGAN PRELUDE — Voluntary in D Minor .... Stanley

PROCESSIONAL HYMN — *"The Church's One Foundation"* .... No. 380
(The congregation will join in singing on the 2nd stanza)

INVOCATION .... Pastor

PRESENTATION OF THE BUILDING .... Mr. Swanson Jones, Mr. Cecil Bryant

SCRIPTURE READING .... Rev. S. B. Tucker

ORGAN MEDITATION — *"Amazing Grace"*

PRAYER OF DEDICATION .... Rev. Thomas Mabe

HYMN OF DEDICATION — (Tune: *"O Master, Let Me Walk With Thee"*) .. Smith

O God, Who in the yesteryear
Did'st move among Thy people here
And cause their trusting eyes to see
A vision . . . . now reality.

We come before Thy presence now,
In gratitude we humbly bow
To thank Thee that Thy hand hath led
To faithful ones Thy paths to tread.

We stand today on holy ground
And feel their spirits here surround
This edifice of brick and stone . . .
A work that is not ours alone.

But all who shared with hand and heart
To build these walls have had their part.
Thy hand, amid us, wrought, unseen,
To bring fruition to our dream.

We dedicate these walls to Thee,
O let them now a gateway be
To learning of Thee and Thy ways.
Our Father God, we give Thee praise.

WELCOME — RECOGNITIONS .... Pastor

GREETINGS FROM THE LYNCHBURG BAPTIST ASSOCIATION .. Mr. Joseph Johnson, Jr.

OFFERTORY ANTHEM — *"True Thanks"* by Philip Young .... Concord Choir

OFFERTORY .... Clerambault

THE DEDICATION

Pastor: Believing that God has been the Builder of this house through His servants, we offer unto Him our humble and grateful praise, and we acknowledge that, "Except the Lord build the house, they labour in vain that build it."

People: "Bless the Lord, O my soul: and all that is within me, bless his holy name. Bless the Lord, O my soul, and forget not all his benefits."

Pastor: To the glory of God the Father, whose grace is sufficient for all our needs; to the honor of His Son, who in love, and self-sacrifice has secured for us redemption and eternal life; to the praise of the Holy spirit, who illumines, comforts, and strengthens us;

People: **To Thee, the only true God, we gratefully dedicate this building.**

Pastor: With thanksgiving to God for the church, and for the work of His grace within us, enabling us to come to this good hour,

People: **We gladly dedicate this building.**

Pastor: For the worship of God in prayer and praise; for the preaching of the gospel of Jesus Christ; for the teaching of the Holy Scriptures;

People: **We humbly dedicate this building.**

Pastor: For the observance of the Lord's Supper and Baptism; for the comfort of those who mourn; for the encouragement of those who are weak; for the help of those seeking guidance;

People: **We faithfully dedicate this building.**

Pastor: For the evangelization of our community and the world; for the promotion of righteousness; for the battle against evil;

People: **We obediently dedicate this building.**

Pastor: For the extension of Christ's teaching to the whole world; for the exaltation of Christian brotherhood; for the relief of human suffering;

People: **We hopefully dedicate this building.**

Pastor: In the unity of the faith; in the bond of Christian discipleship; in acknowledgement of our affection for the cooperation with other churches;

People: **We joyfully dedicate this building.**

Pastor: In gratitude for the labors and gifts of all who love and serve this church; in loving remembrance of those who have finished their course; with faith in those who will follow us;

People: **We hopefully dedicate this building.**

Unison: **We, the people of this church and congregation, with gratitude, do dedicate ourselves anew to the worship and service of God, through our Lord, Jesus Christ.**

THE DEDICATION ANTHEM —

"O How Amiable Are Thy Dwellings" by Williams . . . . Chancel Choir

O How amiable are thy dwellings: thou Lord of hosts! My soul hath a desire and longing to enter into the courts of the Lord: My heart and my flesh rejoice in the living God. Yea, the sparrow hath found her an house, and the swallow a nest where she may lay her young: even thy altars, O Lord of hosts, my King and my God. Blessed are they that dwell in thy house: They will be always praising thee. The glorious Majesty of the Lord our God be upon us: prosper thou the work of our hands upon us. O prosper thou our handy-work, O prosper thou our handy-work. O God, our help in ages past, Our hope for years to come, Our shelter from the stormy blast, And our eternal home.

THE DEDICATION SERMON . . . . Rev. Charles Fuller

HYMN — *"I Love Thy Kingdom, Lord"* . . . . No. 382

BENEDICTION . . . . Rev. Curtis P. Cleveland

ORGAN POSTLUDE — *"The Old Hundredth Psalm Tune"*

A Service Of Worship

Celebrating the Marriage of

Amelia Ann Brookshire
and
Robert Glenn Sherer, Jr.

First Baptist Church
North Wilkesboro, North Carolina

The Organ Prelude

Jesu, Joy of Man's Desiring . . . . Bach
Fugue In G Major . . . . Bach
Toccata and Fugue in D Minor . . . . Bach
Grand Choeur Dialogue . . . . Gigout
Psalm XIX . . . . Marcello
In Christ There Is No East or West . . . . Reinagle

*The Processional
Tune and Air In D . . . . Purcell

*The Call To Worship . . . . Mr. Mendenhall

*The Hymn of Praise
Joyful, Joyful We Adore Thee . . . . Beethoven

*The Prayer of Invocation and Thanksgiving . . . . Mr. Mendenhall

A LITANY ON THE MEANING OF MARRIAGE . . . . Mr. Mendenhall

THE MINISTER . . . . Genesis 2:18, 21-24; 1, 27-28
Then the Lord God said, "It is not good that the man should be alone. I will make
him a helper fit for him." So the Lord God caused a deep sleep to fall upon the
man, and while he slept took one of his ribs and closed up its place with flesh; and
the rib which the Lord God had taken from the man He made into a woman and
brought her to the man. Then the man said, "This at last is bone of my bones and
flesh of my flesh; she shall be called Woman, because she was taken out of Man."
Therefore a man leaves his father and his mother and cleaves to his wife, and they
become one flesh. So God created man in his own image, in the image of God He
created him; male and female He created them. And God blessed them, and God
said to them. "Be fruitful and multiply, and fill the earth and subdue it; and have
dominion over the fish of the sea and over the birds of the air and over every living
thing that moves upon the earth."

THE CONGREGATION:
*As Christians, we affirm that marriage is a sacred relationship, instituted by God as
part of his original plan of creation.*

THE MINISTER: . . . . Matthew 19: 4-6
Jesus answered, "Have you not read that He who made them from the beginning made them male and female, and said, 'For this reason a man shall leave his father and mother and be joined to his wife, and the two shall become one'? So they are no longer two but one. What therefore God has joined together, let no man put asunder."

THE CONGREGATION:
We affirm that marriage as a sacred covenant cannot be destroyed externally, and should not be broken by man.

THE MINISTER: . . . . Ephesians 5: 21-25
Be subject to one another out of reverence for Christ. Wives, be subject to your husbands, as to the Lord. For the husband is the head of the wife as Christ is the head of the church, his body, and is himself its Savior. As the church is subject to Christ, so let wives also be subject in everything to their husbands. Husbands, love your wives, as Christ loved the church, and gave himself up for her.

THE CONGREGATION:
We affirm that God's love is perfected in Jesus Christ with Whom this marriage covenant is made.

THE MINISTER: . . . . Ephesians 5: 28-30, 35
Even so husbands should love their wives as their own bodies. He who loves his wife loves himself. For no man ever hates his own flesh, but nourishes and cherishes it, as Christ does the church, because we are members of His body. Let each one of you love his wife as himself, and let the wife see that she respects her husband.

THE CONGREGATION:
We affirm that Christian marriage is a relationship characterized by mutual respect, trust, and love.

UNISON: . . . . I John 4: 8-9, 11-12
He who does not love does not know God; for God is love. In this the love of God was made manifest among us, that God sent his only Son into the world, so that we might live through him. Beloved, if God so loved us, also ought to love one another. No man has ever seen God; if we love one another, God abides in us and his love is perfected in us.

The Contemporary Word . . . . Dr. Seymour

* *The Gloria Patri*

The Solemnization of Holy Marriage . . . . Dr. Seymour

**The Hymn of Thanksgiving*
Now Thank We All Our God . . . . Mendelssohn

*The Benediction . . . . Mr. Mendenhall

*The Recessional
Tocatta, Suite Gothique . . . . Boellmann

* Congregation Standing

The Congregation is cordially invited to attend the reception immediately following the service.

Resource 20

<u>AN ORDER OF WORSHIP IN CORPORATE MORNING PRAYER</u>

<u>IN THY PRESENCE</u> (The Minister) Archbishop Trench

<u>CALLS TO WORSHIP</u>

Minister: No man hath seen God at any time. If we love one another, God dwelleth in us, and his love is perfected in us... God is love; and he that dwelleth in love dwelleth in God, and God in him.

People: Let all mortal flesh keep silence, in fear and trembling stand; Ponder nothing earthly minded, for with blessing in His hand, God within His temple dwelleth, Our full homage doth demand.

Minister: God resisteth the proud, and giveth grace to the humble. Humble yourselves therefore under the mighty hand of God, that He may exalt you in due time: casting all your care upon him; for he careth for you.

<u>INVOCATION</u> (The Minister)

Let us pray.

Almighty God, our heavenly Father; receive us in this morning hour as we offer ourselves anew to thee in body, soul, and spirit. Let not this day pass except it leave its benediction with us. Give to us the still and quiet heart. Speak to us thy truth, that we may glorify thee; through Jesus Christ our Lord. Amen.

<u>COLLECT FOR PURITY</u> (The Minister and People in Unison)

Almighty God, unto whom all hearts are open, all desires known, and from whom no secrets are hid; cleanse the thoughts of our hearts by the inspiration of thy Holy Spirit, that we may perfectly love thee, and worthily magnify thy holy name; through Christ our Lord. Amen.

<u>RESPONSIVE PRAYER</u> (Minister and People)

Minister: Search me, O God, and know my heart.
People: Try me, and know my thoughts.

Minister: And see if there be any wicked way in me.
People: And lead me in the way everlasting.

Minister: Lord, lift thou up the light of thy countenance upon us.
People: Out of the depths have I cried unto thee, O Lord.

Minister: Lord, hear my voice.
People: Let thine ears be attentive to the voice of my supplications.

Minister: If thou, Lord, shouldst mark iniquities, O Lord, who shall stand.

People: But there is forgiveness with thee, that thou mayest be feared.

CONFESSION OF SIN (Minister and People in Unison)

Seeing that we have a great high priest that is passed into the heavens, Jesus the Son of God, let us come boldly unto the throne of grace, that we may obtain mercy and find grace to help in time of need.

Lord God, almighty and everlasting Father, we acknowledge and confess before thy holy majesty that we are poor sinners, born in corruption, inclined to evil, unable by ourselves to do what is good, and that every day and in many ways we transgress thy holy commandments, so bringing upon us by thy just judgment condemnation and death.

Yet, O Lord, our sorrow is deep that we have offended thee, and with true repentance we condemn ourselves and our sins, humbly imploring thy grace and beseeching thee to provide for our need. Have mercy upon us, most gracious God; Father of mercies, pardon our sins for the love of Jesus Christ, thy Son, our Lord. Blot out our stains; grant unto us and continually increase in us the gifts of thy Holy Spirit, to the end that, acknowledging more and more our faults and being deeply grieved thereby, we may renounce them with all our heart and bring forth fruits of righteousness and holiness, acceptable to thee through Jesus Christ our Lord. Amen. --John Calvin and Theodore Beza

THE ASSURANCE OF GOD'S PARDON (The Minister)

Who is like unto God, that pardoneth iniquity and passeth by the transgression of his heritage? He retaineth not his anger forever, because he delighteth in mercy. He will turn again and have compassion upon us; he will tread our iniquities under foot and cast all our sins into the depths of the sea.

O God, from whom all holy desyres, all good counsayles, and all iuste workes do procede: Geue unto thy seruauntes that peace, which the world cannot geue; that both our hartes maye be sette to obey thy commaundementes, and also that by thee we being defended from the feare of oure enemies, may passe oure time in rest and quietness; throughe the merites of Jesu Christe our sauiour. Amen.
--From the First Prayerbook of Edward VI

PRAYER FOR PARDON (The Minister)

O Lord, we beseech thee, absolve thy people from their offenses, that through thy bountiful goodness we may be delivered from the bonds of those sins which by our frailty we have committed. Grant this, O heavenly Father, for Jesus Christ's sake, our blessed Lord and Saviour. Amen

A MORNING MEDITATION ON THE LORD'S PRAYER

OUR FATHER, WHO ART IN HEAVEN,

Help me to believe this day that there is power to lift me up which is stronger than all the things that hold me down.

HALLOWED BE THY NAME.

Help me to be sensitive to what is beautiful, and responsive to what is good, so that day by day I may grow more sure of the holiness of life in which I want to trust.

THY KINGDOM COME.

Help me to be quick to see, and ready to encourage, whatever brings the better meaning of God into that which otherwise might be the common round of the uninspired day.

THY WILL BE DONE, ON EARTH AS IT IS IN HEAVEN.

Help me to believe that the ideals of the spirit are not a far-off dream, but a power to command my loyalty and direct my life here on our real earth.

GIVE US THIS DAY OUR DAILY BREAD.

Open the way for me to earn an honest living without anxiety, but never let me forget the needs of others, and make me want only that benefit for myself which will also be their gain.

AND FORGIVE US OUR TRESPASSES, AS WE FORGIVE THOSE WHO TRESPASS AGAINST US.

Make me patient and sympathetic with the shortcomings of others, especially of those I love; and keep me sternly watchful only of my own. Let me never grow hard with the unconscious cruelty of those who measure themselves by mean standards, and so think they have excelled. Keep my eyes lifted to the highest, so that I may be humbled; and seeing the failures of others be forgiving, because I know how much there is of which I need to be forgiven.

AND LEAD US NOT INTO TEMPTATION, BUT DELIVER US FROM EVIL.

Let me not go carelessly this day within the reach of any evil I cannot resist, but if the path of duty I must go where temptation is, give me strength of spirit to meet it without fear.

FOR THINE IS THE KINGDOM, AND THE POWER, AND THE GLORY FOR EVER AND EVER. AMEN.

And so in my heart may I carry the knowledge that thy greatness is above me and around me, and that thy grace through Jesus Christ my Master is sufficient for all my needs. Amen.

(This meditation comes from Dr. Walter Russell Bowie, "Lift Up Your Hearts," The Macmillan Company, 1939, p. 3.)

Resource 22

Christian Service of Worship

PRELUDE   Mr. Sloan

"world, i am youth"   Poem

PRAYER   "We Give Thee Thanks"

> Leader: O give Thanks to the Lord, for he is good.
> Youth: We thank thee for hamburgers with onions,
>   for french fries and cokes,
>   For big, juicy pizzas, for ice cold milk,
>   For salted cashew nuts, for hot, buttered rolls.
>   For delicious apples, and milk cheddar cheese.

> Leader: O give thanks to the Lord, for he is good.
> Youth: We thank thee for knits, and rough-textured tweeds,
>   For blue jeans, tennis shoes, and big sloppy sweatshirts,
>   For cashmere sweaters, and Italian-made sandals,
>   For warm, wooly knee socks, and soft, roomy loafers.

> Leader: O give thanks to the Lord, for he is good.
> Youth; We thank thee for the feeling that binds us to one another,
>   though we're too embarrassed to call it love.
>   For the person who is close enough to understand us, accept
>   us, and tell us what we're really like.
>   And, for the person who offers his ear when we need to be
>   heard.
>   We thank thee, Father, for our human parents, who mean
>   well, even do well, more than we would like to admit.

> Leader: O give thanks to the Lord, for he is good.
> Youth: We thank thee for the church which reminds us of thy claim
>   upon our lives in spite of our own wishes to live unto
>   ourselves.
>   For the wonder and awe of our own person and for the hope
>   and promise of what we can become in you and with each
>   other.
>   And above all, we thank thee for the love of Christ, and
>   the clue of thy presence in this crazy, mixed-up, won-
>   derful world. Amen.

HYMN 293   "LOVE IS THE THEME"   Congregation

The Word For Today

> Leader: Our world hears about love,
> People: But it does not know love.

> Leader: Our world seeks desperately for love,
> People: But it does not know that for which it seeks.
>   Our world needs love, needs to love and to be loved.

> Leader: Scripture: John 3:16, I John 3:18, 4:1-12, 16
>   (Good News For Modern Man)

Celebration of Easter

Eleven o'clock a.m.

As you enter the sanctuary, let talking cease and prayer begin.

The Organ:—"Prelude on "O Sacred Head, now wounded" *Johannes Brahms*

The Crucifixion

A Call from the Cross . . . . Minister

The Scripture:—Mark 15:16-20; 24-30 . . . Minister and Choirs

Litany of Confession . . . . Minister and Congregation

Minister: Men and women mocked Him and spit on Him and hit Him.

People: He died, and they buried Him in Jerusalem.

Minister: Men and women talked against Him and nailed Him to a cross.

People: He died, and they buried Him in a borrowed tomb.

Minister: Christ is still dying in a torn world, a hate-filled world, a prejudiced world.

People: He continues to choose to suffer the cross for the redemption of sick and lost mankind. He suffers when men and women choose to bear more than their share of this world's suffering.

Minister: Let all God's people confess. For our personal and private sins;

People: O God, forgive.

Minister: For our wrongs inflicted upon our neighbors;

People: O God, forgive.

Minister: For our part in our world's problems;

People: O God, forgive.

Minister: For our fear in not acting; our blindness to suffering; our willingness to let others do what we ought to do;

People: O God, forgive, and give us courage in our lives and our living.

Pastoral Prayer . . . . Minister

Man's Response

The Resurrection

The Tomb . . . . Youth Choir

Litany of Discovery . . . . Minister and Congregation

Minister: The stone is rolled away!

People: Men have taken away our Lord's body. We don't know what they did with it.

Minister: He is not here. He is risen from the dead!

People: But we saw Him die. We heard Him cry out: Father, forgive them.

Anthem of Celebration:—"Rejoice, my soul! The Lord is Risen!"
The Senior Choir *John T. Lowerty*

The Sermon:—"TRUMPETS IN THE MORNING!" . . . Minister

The Commitment

Prayer of Dedication . . . . Minister

Presentation of Tithes and Offerings

Offertory Anthem:—"Christ is risen!" (John S. B. Monsell) *Maker-Wetzler*
The Combined Choirs

Hymn of Commitment:—"Christ the Lord is risen today" (Charles Wesley)
Number 115 *Traditional Melody*

Benediction . . . . Minister

Choral Response:—"Hallelujah Chorus" (from "Messiah") *George F. Handel*

The Organ:—Voluntary on "Come, ye faithful" *Sullivan-Lowerty*

We express appreciation to the following who participated in this service, but who are not included in the above printed order: Jerry Williams, Robin Smith, David Colvard, and Paul Dell.

Broadcast over Radio Station WSSB (1490)

THE MINISTERS

R. F. Smith, Jr., Pastor

Leath C. Johnson, Minister of Education John T. Lowerty, Minister of Music

Sympathy: We express Christian sympathy to Mrs. T. H. Lindsey in the loss of her sister.

Resource 24

WORKSHEET FOR PLANNING TEAM

Date _____   Theme of Service _____

Staff Position of Planner _____

Invitation to Worship (Changes every 2 months)

Preparation for Worship (Changed every Sunday)

We Enter Into Worship
    Organ Prelude--
    Hymn--
    Invocation--
    Choral Response--
    Organ Interlude--
We Hold Conversation With God
    Scripture--
    Anthem (or other)--
    Choral Response--
    Hymn--
We Enter Into Parternship With God
    Welcome--
    Offertory Sentence--
    Offertory--
    Offering
    Prayer of Dedication--
We Open Our Minds to God's Truth
    Silent Prayer
    Sermon--
We Consecrate Ourselves to God and His Will
    Invitation
    Hymn--
    Benediction--
    Choral Benediction--
    Organ Postlude--

MORNING WORSHIP
May 17, 1970

PENTECOST SUNDAY
+
PREPARATION FOR WORSHIP
10:50 a. m.

As this service begins, let me recognize that my standards
are high, my criticisms sharp, and my need fundamental.
Save me from the cult of mediocrity, in this service, and
in my own life.

The Prelude: "Adagio from Sonata II" .   .   Mendelssohn
The Chiming of the Hour . . . . . . Mr. Sloan
+   +   +

THE SERVICE OF WORSHIP

Aspiration

PROCESSIONAL HYMN 6 . . . . Neander
                "Praise to the Lord"

CONFESSION OF SIN .   . (Unison - Congregation seated)
        Youth Leader - Miss Jane Foster)

Almighty and eternal God, who searchest the hearts of men: We
acknowledge and confess that we have sinned against thee in
thought, word, and deed; that we have not loved thee with all our
heart and soul, and with all our mind and strength; and that
we that we have not loved our neighbors as ourselves. Forgive
us our transgressions and help us to amend our ways; and of
thine eternal goodness direct what we shall be, so that we
may henceforth walk in the way of thy commandments, and do
those things which are worthy in thy sight; through Jesus
Christ our Lord. Amen.

   Leader: Lord, have mercy on us.

   People: Christ, hear our earnest prayer.

   Leader: "Come to me, all who labor and are heavy-laden,
and I will give you rest."

   People: The Lord be praised!

THE GLORIA PATRI .   .   . The Choir and Congregation

                Devotion

Meditation Interlude .   .   .   .   . The Organist
   (Visitors are invited to register on the visitor's card
given you by an usher or found in the back of a pew.)

Reading of the Scriptures . . . . . Acts 2:1-4
(New English Bible)

The Pastoral Prayer and the Lord's Prayer

Solo . . . . Mrs. James Lovette
"I Will Magnify Thee" Bach

Instruction

THE SERMON . . . . Mr. Laymon

Title: "A God Sent "Happening"
Text: "—you are a letter written not with ink, but with
the Spirit of the living God, written not on stone
tablets, but on the pages of the human heart."
(II Corinthians 3:3)

Dedication

The Offertory Sentence . . . . Exodus 35:21

"—and they brought the Lord's offering to the work of the
tabernacle of the congregation, and for all his service."

The Offertory Anthem . . . . . . McCormick
"God Is A Spirit"

God is a spirit; and they that worship Him must worship Him
in spirit and in truth.
I know that my Messiah cometh, And when he is come, He will
tell us all things.

THE DOXOLOGY . . . . . . The Choir and Congregation

The Prayer of Dedication

Fellowship

Invitation to DISCIPLESHIP

HYMN 170 . . . . Gottschalk
"HOLY GHOST, WITH LIGHT DIVINE"

(This is the time for Public Commitment to Christ and His
Church, when we offer to Him ourselves as well as our resources. Persons who desire to request membership in this
congregation are invited to come forward to be welcomed as
the hymn is sung.)

The Benediction and Choral Response
The Chiming of the Hour . . . . The Organist

The Postlude . . . "Allegro Maestoso-Sonata II"

+   +   +